Standards Review Workbook

HOLT

California Social Studies United States History Independence to 1914

HOLT, RINEHART AND WINSTON

A Harcourt Education Company

Orlando • **Austin** • New York • San Diego • Toronto • London

Printed in the United States of America

ISBN 0-03-041853-4

24 25 26   1186   18 17 16

4500580413

Contents

Contents

Name ______________________ Class ______________ Date ____________

History–Social Science Grade 6 — Standard 6.1 Review

STANDARDS REVIEW

HSS 6.1 Students describe what is known through archaeological studies of the early physical and cultural development of humankind from the Paleolithic era to the agricultural revolution.

Many scientists think the first modern humans appeared in Africa about 200,000 years ago. These early humans lived during a time called the Stone Age. Early humans gradually developed tools, such as sharpened stones for processing food, flint axes, and spears. These people were hunter-gatherers. They hunted animals and gathered wild plants for survival. They learned to use fire. These early people also developed language and created art, including cave paintings and carvings.

During the Paleolithic Era, early people began to move around. From Africa, scientists believe humans went first to Asia. Early peoples eventually spread over thousands of years to Europe, Australia, North America, and South America. People learned to sew clothing from animal skins, build shelters, create new and better tools, and make pottery. A major change occurred about 5,000 years ago in Southwest Asia, but later in other parts of the world. There, people learned how to grow food crops by planting seeds. They also learned to raise animals, rather than following herds. This huge shift from food gathering to food producing is called the Agricultural, or Neolithic, Revolution.

STANDARDS PRACTICE

DIRECTIONS Read each question and circle the letter of the best response.

1 Which statement does not describe hunter-gatherers?

A They lived during the Stone Age.
B They developed tools.
C They made cave paintings.
D They grew crops by planting seeds.

2 Where did the first humans live?

A Asia
B Africa
C Australia
D Europe

3 In the Agricultural Revolution, people first learned to

A raise animals.
B use fire.
C make carvings.
D sharpen stones.

STANDARDS REVIEW

HSS 6.2 Students analyze the geographic, political, economic, religious, and social structures of the early civilizations of Mesopotamia, Egypt, and Kush.

In several parts of the world, bands of hunter-gatherers settled down in farming settlements. Over time, their cultures became more complex. Most early civilizations grew up along rivers. Three of the earliest were at the eastern end of the Mediterranean Sea. Mesopotamia lay between the Tigris and Euphrates Rivers. In this fertile region, farmers grew crops and raised livestock. Cities appeared between 4000 and 3000 BC. Sumer was the world's first advanced society, with religion, writing, technology, armies, and a social order. Other civilizations, such as Babylonia, Assyria, and Phoenicia, followed Sumer in Mesopotamia.

At about the same time, other people settled along the Nile River in Egypt. Around 3100 BC, the kingdom of Egypt arose. Ruled by a pharaoh, ancient Egyptians developed a society with a strict class order, a religion with many gods, trade, art, a powerful military, and a system of writing called hieroglyphics. Egyptians were also known for their buildings, including massive temples and pyramids. South of Egypt in Africa, a third early civilization grew up around 2000 BC. It was Kush. Sometimes Kush was dominated by neighboring Egypt, but in the 700s BC, Kush conquered Egypt. Kush was known for its advanced iron industry, and it had extensive trade relations with other peoples.

STANDARDS PRACTICE

DIRECTIONS Read each question and circle the letter of the best response.

1 Which civilization did not grow up in Mesopotamia?

A Babylonia
B Assyria
C Kush
D Sumer

2 What is one thing all these civilizations have in common?

A Each had an advanced iron industry.
B Each grew up near a river.
C Each had a system of writing called hieroglyphics.
D Each lay between the Tigris and Euphrates Rivers.

Name ______________________ Class ______________ Date ______________

STANDARDS REVIEW

HSS 6.3 Students analyze the geographic, political, economic, religious, and social structures of the Ancient Hebrews.

The civilization of the Hebrews dates back to Abraham, who settled in Canaan on the Mediterranean Sea between 2000 and 1500 BC. The Hebrews, or Jewish people, endured a period of slavery in Egypt. They were led back to Canaan by Moses around 1200 BC, a journey known as the Exodus. According to the Bible, on this journey God gave Moses a set of laws called the Ten Commandments. The Jews believed that if they obeyed God, followed the Ten Commandments, and valued human life, self-control, and justice, God would look after them. The Jews' religion became known as Judaism. Historians believe it was the first monotheistic religion. Monotheism is the belief in only one God.

Over their history, the Jews have suffered periods of persecution and exile. Their capital, Jerusalem, was destroyed, and many Jews were forced to move away from Israel, their homeland. They were conquered by neighboring peoples, including the Assyrians, Chaldeans, and Romans. Numerous revolts ended in failure. Through difficult times, their faith has remained strong. Jewish values, such as justice, obedience to the law, and education, have been especially influential in Western civilization. Christianity grew from Jewish roots. Judaism also has aspects in common with Islam. Today, Jews live all over the world.

STANDARDS PRACTICE

DIRECTIONS Read each question and circle the letter of the best response.

1 Which of the following statements about the ancient Hebrews is true?

A Theirs was the first monotheistic religion.
B They conquered Egypt.
C They founded the Christian religion.
D Their civilization was started by Moses.

2 Monotheism is

A the belief in the Jewish God.
B the belief in the Ten Commandments.
C the belief in only one God.
D the belief in Abraham and Moses.

3 Which is not a Jewish value?

A justice
B obedience to the law
C education
D tyranny

STANDARDS REVIEW

HSS 6.4 Students analyze the geographic, political, economic, religious, and social structures of the early civilizations of Ancient Greece.

One of the greatest of all ancient civilizations developed in a rocky, mountainous region in the Mediterranean Sea. Around 600 BC, small, independent city-states grew up in Greece. The most important city-state, Athens, soon set up trading colonies and grew more powerful. Early in its history, Athens was ruled by aristocrats and then by a king called a tyrant. Around 500 BC, however, a new form of government was invented in Athens—a democracy. In Athens's democracy, citizens assembled to vote on matters that affected their city. All modern democratic countries trace their roots to ancient Athens in Greece.

Athens flourished for only a short time. During its golden age, it gave the world some of its greatest literature, philosophy, history, art, architecture, mathematics, and science. Greeks also created a rich mythology to explain the world. In the mid-400s BC, however, Athens lost a destructive war with another city-state, the military state of Sparta. The war weakened all of Greece, and within 100 years, Greece was conquered by Macedonia, a small country north of Greece. However, the leader of Macedonia, Alexander the Great, admired Greek culture tremendously. He spread this culture throughout Asia as he built a huge empire. Through Alexander, Greek culture was preserved.

STANDARDS PRACTICE

DIRECTIONS Read each question and circle the letter of the best response.

1 Democracy was invented in

A Macedonia.
(**B**) Athens.
C Sparta.
D Rome.

2 How did Alexander preserve Greek culture?

A He created a rich mythology.
B He became a king called a tyrant.
C He conquered Sparta.
(**D**) He spread it throughout his empire.

3 In Greek democracy,

A all people voted.
B men and women voted.
(**C**) citizens voted.
D wealthy people voted.

STANDARDS REVIEW

HSS 6.5 Students analyze the geographic, political, economic, religious, and social structures of the early civilizations of India.

India is separated by mountains, deserts, and seas from the rest of Asia. This isolation helped India develop its own special civilizations. The earliest civilization in India was the Harappan. Like other early civilizations, it grew up along a river, the Indus. By the 1200s BC, the Harappans had been replaced by the Aryans. The Aryans were a people from the north. These people gave their language, Sanskrit, and their religion, Brahmanism, to India. Brahmanism divided society into strict classes called castes. The caste system determined almost everything about a person's life. Brahmanism developed into Hinduism, the religion of today's India. Hindus believe in many gods, who are all different parts of one god. Hindus also believe in reincarnation, or rebirth into another life form, and the importance of doing one's duty. India is also the birthplace of another world religion. In the 500s BC, a man named Siddhartha created Buddhism. Buddhists search for enlightenment, or wisdom, and nirvana, a state of perfect peace.

In the 320s BC, a great leader named Asoka united most of India in one kingdom. He ruled by Buddhist principles, trying to improve the lives of his people. Under Asoka and other kings, India developed a rich culture. India excelled in art, architecture, literature, and mathematics.

STANDARDS PRACTICE

DIRECTIONS Read each question and circle the letter of the best response.

1 Which is not a Hindu belief?

A isolationism
B reincarnation
C the importance of doing one's duty
D belief in many gods, who are all different parts of one god

2 Who were the Aryans?

A the creators of Buddhism
B founders of a state of perfect peace
C leaders who ruled by Buddhist principles
D a people from the north who invaded India

3 For what is Asoka known?

A He created Buddhism.
B He named the Indus River.
C He found enlightenment, or wisdom.
D He was a king who ruled by Buddhist principles

STANDARDS REVIEW

HSS 6.6 Students analyze the geographic, political, economic, religious, and social structures of the early civilizations of China.

East of India, another great culture grew up along major rivers. China is a vast and varied land, and the country's first civilization was located along the Huang He, or Yellow River, in northern China. About 1500 BC, a group of rulers called the Shang had gained control. Among the Shang's achievements was China's first writing system. The next rulers, called the Zhou, solidified control over more of China, but eventually weakened. During a period of social chaos in the 500s BC, a man named Confucius looked for solutions to China's problems. He called for people to behave morally, be loyal, and perform their proper roles. His ideas are still influential today. Another set of ideas, called Daoism, suggested that people should live in harmony with nature.

The next dynasty, or group of related rulers, was the Qin. Its great emperor Shi Huangdi was able to unify all of China with his ruthless policies. He also built a Great Wall to protect China from its enemies. Rulers of the Han dynasty took power around 200 BC. They adopted Confucianism to create a strong central government. Art and learning thrived under the Han. They also opened trade routes to other countries, including the Silk Road across Asia to Europe. Also at this time, Buddhism arrived in China from India.

STANDARDS PRACTICE

DIRECTIONS Read each question and circle the letter of the best response.

1 Which is not a belief of Confucianism?

A People should behave morally.
B People should perform their proper roles.
C People should live in harmony with nature.
D People should be loyal.

2 Which dynasty created a strong central government in China?

A Qin
B Han
C Shang
D Zhou

3 Who built a Great Wall?

A Confucius
B Zhou
C Shi Huangdi
D Shang

STANDARDS REVIEW

HSS 6.7 Students analyze the geographic, political, economic, religious, and social structures during the development of Rome.

The city of Rome lies on a river near the western coast of Italy, a peninsula that extends out into the Mediterranean Sea. This beneficial location helped Rome become the greatest civilization of the ancient world. Rome was founded in the 700s BC and became a republic in 509. Over centuries, the Roman Republic created a written constitution, a system of laws, and a three-part government with executive, legislative, and judicial branches. Rome gradually defeated and conquered more of its neighbors until it ruled a large area. After many years of social and political disorder, however, Augustus seized power in 27 BC. Rome became an empire.

Under its emperors, Rome expanded into a vast empire that stretched from Britain to Mesopotamia. The Roman Empire was united by an extensive road network, a common money system, and its magnificent army. People throughout the empire felt proud to be Roman citizens. But even this great empire eventually weakened and fell in the AD 400s. Its many contributions to the world live on. Its laws, science, architecture, literature, and art are still admired. Its language, Latin, is used today. Yet another contribution of Rome is the preservation and expansion of Christianity. The religion was born in the Roman Empire, and within a few centuries became the empire's official religion.

STANDARDS PRACTICE

DIRECTIONS Read each question and circle the letter of the best response.

1 What form of government did Rome have before it became an empire?

A dictatorship
B democracy
C monarchy
D republic

2 Which was not one of Rome's lasting contributions to the world?

A democracy
B laws
C architecture
D Christianity

3 Which helped unite the Roman Empire?

A the legislative branch of government
B a common money system
C its architecture
D pride in being a Greek citizen

STANDARDS REVIEW

HSS 7.1 Students analyze the causes and effects of the vast expansion and ultimate disintegration of the Roman Empire.

Between the 700s BC and the AD 100s, Rome grew from a tiny village to a huge empire. Several factors helped Rome create its vast empire. Written laws protected the rights of Roman citizens. An extensive road network for good communications, a common money system, and a magnificent army also strengthened the Roman Empire. Allowing conquered people to become Roman citizens made them loyal to Rome.

Yet the empire also faced serious problems as time passed. By the end of the 100s, emperors began to give up land Rome had conquered. The empire had grown too large to govern effectively. Emperors divided it into eastern and western halves. Outsiders known as barbarians attacked the borders of the empire. There were not enough farmers to grow food because so many people were in the army. Emperors were ineffective, and political leaders formed private armies to fight each other for power. Disease often swept through the empire, and economic problems led to growing weakness. Taxes and prices soared. Political corruption increased, Rome's dependence on slaves grew, and schools closed. Barbarians even attacked the city of Rome itself in 410. By the end of the 400s, Rome had fallen. The torch of Roman civilization was passed to the eastern part of the empire, known as the Byzantine Empire. Its capital Constantinople became the center of a new and influential civilization that combined Roman and Greek values.

STANDARDS PRACTICE

DIRECTIONS Read the question and circle the letter of the best response.

1 How did emperors address the problem of the empire's large size?

A They formed private armies.
B They divided it into eastern and western halves.
C They combined Roman and Greek values.
D They created a money system.

2 Which statement about the Byzantine Empire is true?

A It combined Roman and barbarian values.
B Its written laws protected the rights of Roman citizens.
C It was the eastern part of the Roman Empire.
D It was the western part of the Roman Empire.

STANDARDS REVIEW

HSS 7.2 Students analyze the geographic, political, economic, religious, and social structures of the civilizations of Islam in the Middle Ages.

In the early AD 600s, a new religion was born in the desert country of Arabia. Islam is based on the teachings of Muhammad, whom Muslims believe was the prophet of God, or Allah. Islam, like Judaism and Christianity, is a monotheistic religion. Muslims believe in promoting justice, praying daily, helping the poor, and obeying Allah's commands, found in the Qur'an. Muhammad and his followers gradually took political control of parts of Arabia. After Muhammad's death in 632, Muslims expanded their empire to include most of the Middle East, northern Africa, and even parts of Europe. A Muslim kingdom was established in Spain in the mid-700s. Eventually, Islam reached from East Asia to Morocco, from Africa to India and Afghanistan.

Different Muslim empires, such as the Safavid Persian, Mughal Indian, and Ottoman Turkish, flourished throughout the Middle Ages. Arab Muslim merchants traded with people in China, India, Africa, and Europe, helping spread Muslim ideas and the Arabic language. A rich cultural life grew up in great cities like Baghdad and Cordoba, Spain. Muslim rulers usually practiced religious tolerance, which added to the cultural richness of their empires. Muslim scholars helped preserve ancient Greek writings lost in the West. Muslim scientists made important advances in astronomy, geography, mathematics, and medicine. Writers and artists created unique Islamic works of art.

STANDARDS PRACTICE

DIRECTIONS Read the question and circle the letter of the best response.

1 Muslim scholars and artists did all of the following except

A preserve ancient Greek writings.

B create unique Islamic works of art.

C preserve written Roman laws.

D make important advances in astronomy and geography.

2 What is one way Islam is like Judaism and Christianity?

A It is also a monotheistic religion.

B It was also founded by Muhammad.

C It also arose in the desert country of Arabia.

D It also uses the New and Old Testaments.

STANDARDS REVIEW

HSS 7.3 Students analyze the geographic, political, economic, religious, and social structures of the civilizations of China in the Middle Ages.

China endured several centuries of social and political unrest from AD 220 to 589. These years are known as the Period of Disunion. It ended when a new dynasty, or group of related rulers, gained power. In 618, the Tang began their 300 years of rule. With China reunited, the Tang period was a golden age for China. It was able to conquer much of Central Asia and Vietnam. Another key event of this period was the spread of Buddhism. During the unrest, many Chinese sought comfort in Buddhism. With the return of order, Buddhism continued to grow. Missionaries took it from China to Japan, Korea, and other lands.

The Tang and following Song periods were times of important advances in agriculture, trade, art, literature, and technology. Several important Chinese inventions of the time are woodblock printing, gunpowder, the magnetic compass, and paper money. Another important development was a return to Confucian values. Confucianism led the Song rulers to create a powerful class of government officials. These officials were especially trained and selected to provide good public service. In the 1200s, China was conquered by a people called the Mongols and their leader Genghis Khan. During Mongol rule and later, China undertook huge building projects, expanded trade with Europe and the Middle East, and also sent expeditions to explore the world outside China.

STANDARDS PRACTICE

DIRECTIONS Read the question and circle the letter of the best response.

1 A key event of the Tang period was

A the creation of a powerful class of government officials.

B expeditions to explore the world outside China.

C the rule of Genghis Khan.

D the spread of Buddhism in China and beyond.

2 All of the following are Chinese inventions except

A the magnetic compass.

B guns.

C gunpowder.

D paper money.

STANDARDS REVIEW

HSS 7.4 Students analyze the geographic, political, economic, religious, and social structures of the sub-Saharan civilizations of Ghana and Mali in Medieval Africa.

Great empires also arose in Africa. The center of West Africa's first civilizations was the Niger River. This huge region contains varied landforms and climates, as well as resources like fertile farmland, salt, and gold. Growing from humble beginnings, Africa's first great empire used trade to gain control over much of West Africa. This empire was Ghana. By the AD 800s it controlled trade routes heading north and south. After several centuries, Ghana weakened and was replaced by the empire of Mali. Mali too grew rich on trade. It also became a great center of learning and of the Islamic religion and the Arabic language, which the rulers of Mali adopted in the 1300s. Mali's imperial capital of Timbuktu became famous throughout the Muslim world. A third great empire, the Songhai, arose in the late 1400s. Also Muslim, the Songhai Empire became a cultural and trading center. The key to their prosperity was control of the trade routes that crossed the dangerous Sahara Desert to the north. An important element of all West African trade was human slaves.

Life in all the West African civilizations was centered on the village and family relationships. Each family member had his or her own duties and responsibilities. Culture was shared orally through stories told by older members of the family group.

STANDARDS PRACTICE

DIRECTIONS Read the question and circle the letter of the best response.

1 All of the following were important West African empires except

A Sahara.
B Songhai.
C Ghana.
D Mali.

2 Which statement about family and village life in West Africa is true?

A All villages were located on the Niger River.
B Life was centered on workplace relationships.
C All families engaged in trans-Saharan trade.
D Culture was shared orally by older members of the family.

STANDARDS REVIEW

HSS 7.5 Students analyze the geographic, political, economic, religious, and social structures of the civilizations of Medieval Japan.

Japan's civilization has been shaped by two important geographic factors. It is an island, which allowed it to develop its own culture. On the other hand, however, Japan is very close to mainland nations like China and Korea. Both have influenced Japan's development. Around AD 600, a leader named Prince Shotoku decided Japan should adopt more Chinese ideas. Japanese learned about written language, Confucianism, and the importance of correct behavior within the family. Shotoku also made Buddhism, introduced from Korea, more popular in Japan. In 794 a great era of artistic and literary achievement known as the Heian began. Among the works of this period was one of the world's first novels, *The Tale of Genji*, by Lady Murasaki Shikibu. Also during the Heian period, new forms of Buddhism developed.

Toward the end of the Heian period, Japanese society became unruly. Large landowners called daimyo hired samurai, or trained professional warriors, to protect them. Samurai lived disciplined lives and followed a strict code of honor called bushido. Even today, many Japanese admire the values of the samurai. At about the same time, the emperor became a weak figurehead. Japan's real ruler was a military commander called the shogun. The shoguns ruled Japan for several centuries. They feared outside ideas could weaken their power. As a result, Japan became isolated from the rest of the world until the 1800s.

STANDARDS PRACTICE

DIRECTIONS Read the question and circle the letter of the best response.

1 Which geographic factor had a strong influence on Japan's development?

A its frequent earthquakes
B its tall mountains
C its closeness to mainland nations
D the policies of Prince Shotoku

2 Trained professional warriors were known as

A shoguns.
B daimyo.
C bushido.
D samurai.

3 What did Japan gain from Korea?

A Buddhism
B shoguns
C Confucianism
D Heian culture

STANDARDS REVIEW

HSS 7.6 Students analyze the geographic, political, economic, religious, and social structures of the civilizations of Medieval Europe.

The Middle Ages is the period following the fall of the western Roman Empire. It lasted from about 500 to about 1500. After Rome fell, Europe had no central authority. During this time, the spread of the Christian Church helped bring some unity and authority to Europe. Christianity was spread by missionaries sent by the pope from Italy to the far corners of Europe. Monks also taught people about Christianity by running schools, preserving writings, and advising local rulers. Threats such as Viking invasions led to the development of a system for protection. It was called feudalism. In return for land, knights promised to be loyal and help nobles fight. Feudalism made possible the manor system. Manors, on which most people lived, included a castle, village, church, and farm fields.

Numerous conflicts raged during the Middle Ages. Popes and kings battled for political power. European Christians battled Muslims who controlled the Holy Land and Spain. Throughout the Middle Ages, the Catholic Church shaped society and politics. It ran universities, sponsored artworks, and influenced kings. In England, the beginnings of democracy were found in the Magna Carta, which defined certain legal rights for people. At the end of the Middle Ages, a dreadful plague carried by rats killed as much as one third of the population.

STANDARDS PRACTICE

DIRECTIONS Read the question and circle the letter of the best response.

1 Which statement about the Christian Church in the Middle Ages is not correct?

- **A** It helped shape society and politics.
- **B** It made possible the manor system.
- **C** It ran schools and preserved writings.
- **D** It brought unity and authority to Europe.

2 Which statement about feudalism is true?

- **A** It started as a system for protection.
- **B** The pope controlled it.
- **C** It was outlined in the Magna Carta.
- **D** It taught people about Christianity.

STANDARDS REVIEW

HSS 7.7 Students compare and contrast the geographic, political, economic, religious, and social structures of the Meso-American and Andean civilizations.

Mesoamerica is the region that includes southern Mexico and the northern countries of Central America. The first great civilization to appear in Mesoamerica was the Maya. Starting about AD 250, the Maya built up a great trading society and many large cities. Trade goods of the Maya included crops like cotton, rubber, and chocolate and minerals such as jade and obsidian, a black rock useful for making tools. The Maya built magnificent temples for worship, made advances in science and mathematics, and developed a complex social system. Around AD 900, however, their civilization declined and disappeared. Historians are not sure why.

In the 1400s, another rich and powerful civilization, the Aztec, developed in central Mexico. Their capital city of Tenochtitlán was one of the world's largest cities, with floating gardens and enormous markets. Aztec society placed king and nobles at the top, and Aztec religion tried to explain the natural world. Like the Maya, they were able to use science to make a calendar. A third great empire dominated the Andes Mountains in South America. The Inca Empire reached its height in the early 1500s. They established trading networks and an official language for the empire. Like the other two societies, the Incas had a rich oral tradition. Both the Aztecs and the Incas met the same fate. They were conquered by Spanish invaders in the 1500s.

STANDARDS PRACTICE

DIRECTIONS Read the question and circle the letter of the best response.

1 Which was not an empire in the Americas?

A the Inca
B the Maya
C the Aztec
D the Mexicans

2 What did the three empires have in common?

A They were destroyed by the Spanish.
B They dominated the Andes.
C They were trading societies.
D They were in Mesoamerica.

STANDARDS REVIEW

HSS 7.8 Students analyze the origins, accomplishments, and geographic diffusion of the Renaissance.

In the late 1300s, a new spirit took hold in Italy. An emphasis on human value and achievement began to balance the medieval focus on God. This new focus, called humanism, was based in part on the rediscovery of classical Greek and Roman writings. This reawakened interest in education, science, and art in the late 1300s was known as the Renaissance, or "rebirth." The Renaissance was also encouraged by increased trade with other parts of the world. The reopening of the old Silk Road between Europe and China helped bring new ideas to Italian cities such as Venice, Milan, and Genoa.

However, the center of the Italian Renaissance was the city of Florence. There, wealthy bankers and others supported great artists, including Michelangelo and Leonardo da Vinci. From Florence, Renaissance ideas spread throughout Italy and into northern Europe. This spread of ideas was made easier by advances in technology. One of the key inventions was the printing press of Johann Gutenberg of Germany. His press made the printing of books, including Bibles in the vernacular, or the commonly spoken languages, much faster and easier. The Renaissance also saw great advances in science, astronomy, engineering, mathematics, cartography (mapmaking), and human anatomy. Great writers of the Renaissance include the Italian poet Dante and the English playwright William Shakespeare.

STANDARDS PRACTICE

DIRECTIONS Read the question and circle the letter of the best response.

1 The meaning of the word Renaissance is

A rebirth.
B return.
C humanism.
D advance.

2 Which statement about the Renaissance is not true?

A It was encouraged by increased trade.
B It was based on the rediscovery of Greek and Roman writings.
C It was brought to Europe from China.
D It saw great advances in science, art, and literature.

Name ______________________ Class ______________ Date ______________

History–Social Science Grade 7 — Standard 7.9 Review

STANDARDS REVIEW

HSS 7.9 Students analyze the historical developments of the Reformation.

By the late Renaissance, some people had become dissatisfied with the Catholic Church. They felt it had grown too rich and become too involved in politics. They believed it was neglecting its spiritual responsibilities. One man who felt this way was the German monk Martin Luther. In 1517, he announced his reform plan for the church, known as the Ninety-Five Theses. Luther claimed that people did not need to give money to the church to be saved. Believing in God and living by the Bible was enough. Other reformers, such as John Calvin, also proposed changes in church practice. Eventually these and others broke with the Catholic Church and helped form new churches. This break is called the Reformation. The new churches that were created are known as Protestant Christian churches. Unlike in the Catholic Church, most Protestant church members governed themselves.

While southern Europe remained Catholic, many people in northern Europe became Protestants. The Catholic Church realized that it had to make changes. Its response to the Protestant Reformation is called the Counter-Reformation. Through the late 1500s and 1600s, the Catholic Church worked to strengthen itself and stop the spread of Protestantism. Catholic reforms included new religious orders such as the Jesuits, missionaries, and a series of meetings called the Council of Trent. All three helped revitalize the Catholic Church. A key effect of the religious split in Europe was that parts of the New World became Catholic, while others became mostly Protestant.

STANDARDS PRACTICE

DIRECTIONS Read the question and circle the letter of the best response.

1 The Reformation resulted in

A the end of the Catholic Church.
B the Ninety-Five Theses.
C the creation of Protestant churches.
D the death of Martin Luther.

2 All were part of the Counter-Reformation except

A missionaries.
B the rise of Protestantism.
C the Council of Trent.
D new religious orders.

STANDARDS REVIEW

HSS 7.10 Students analyze the historical developments of the Scientific Revolution and its lasting effect on religious, political, and cultural institutions.

During the 1500s and 1600s, modern science was born. The series of events that led to the birth of modern science is called the Scientific Revolution. Before the Scientific Revolution, most people accepted explanations about nature and the world from ancient authorities or the Catholic Church. Modern science, however, is based on observation of the world to identify facts. Scientists then use their reason to form theories, or explanations of why things occur. The roots of the Scientific Revolution include the writings of ancient Greek thinkers such as Aristotle and the work of medieval Islamic and Jewish scientists. The spirit of humanism and other Renaissance ideas also led scientists to apply their own reason to explaining the world.

New ideas and inventions during the Scientific Revolution changed the nature of knowledge. In astronomy, Nicolaus Copernicus and Galileo helped show that the Sun was at the center of the solar system. In England, Isaac Newton explained ideas such as gravity and motion and developed calculus. Important inventions including the telescope, microscope, and thermometer helped scientists observe nature more closely. Another key development was the scientific method, a step-by-step method for performing research. At the heart of the method are observation and experimentation. This approach to science is based on the ideas of Englishman Francis Bacon and Frenchman René Descartes.

STANDARDS PRACTICE

DIRECTIONS Read the question and circle the letter of the best response.

1 All of the following were roots of the Scientific Revolution except

A the writings of ancient Greek thinkers.
B the Catholic Church.
C the work of Islamic and Jewish scientists.
D humanism and other Renaissance ideas.

2 The central ideas of the scientific method are

A humanism and Judaism.
B observation and experimentation.
C Bacon and the Catholic Church.
D ancient authorities and Islam.

STANDARDS REVIEW

HSS 7.11 Students analyze political and economic change in the sixteenth, seventeenth, and eighteenth centuries (the Age of Exploration, the Enlightenment, and the Age of Reason).

In the 1400s, a new interest in discovery swept across Europe. Improvements in navigation, maps, and shipbuilding helped Europeans explore the world. The Portuguese explored the coast of Africa and sailed onto India. Following Columbus, the Spanish sailed to the New World. The French and English concentrated on North America. As a result of these voyages of discovery, Europeans' ideas of the world changed. An important exchange of culture, religion, languages, plants, and animals took place between the Americas, Europe, Africa, and Asia. Europeans took with them new ideas, plants, animals, and technology. They returned from their explorations with new plants and animals. This increased trade led to a new economic system based on capitalism, in which individuals, not governments, run most businesses.

Another important change occurred at about the same time. During a period called the Enlightenment, people applied reason to philosophy, society, and politics. Enlightenment thinking was based on Greek and Roman ideas, Christianity, the Renaissance, the Reformation, and the Scientific Revolution. The Enlightenment had an especially strong influence on the development of democratic ideas. In both England and its American colonies, the belief that people had certain rights helped create more democratic governments. For example, ideas of Enlightenment thinkers like John Locke and Charles-Louis Montesquieu shaped the Declaration of Independence and the U.S. Constitution.

STANDARDS PRACTICE

DIRECTIONS Read the question and circle the letter of the best response.

1 In capitalism,

A there is increased trade.
B governments, not individuals, run most businesses.
C voyages of discovery are frequent.
D individuals, not governments, run most businesses.

2 All of the following contributed to the Enlightenment except

A the Declaration of Independence.
B Christianity.
C Greek and Roman ideas.
D the Scientific Revolution.

STANDARDS REVIEW

HSS 8.1 Students understand the major events preceding the founding of the nation and relate their significance to the development of American constitutional democracy.

8.1.1 Describe the relationship between the moral and political ideas of the Great Awakening and the development of revolutionary fervor.

The Great Awakening was a religious movement that swept through the American colonies. After years of population growth, religious leaders wanted to spread religious feeling throughout the colonies. In the late 1730s, these ministers began holding revivals. These were emotional gatherings where people came together to hear sermons.

This movement takes its name from the "great awakening" colonists experienced in their religious lives. It changed colonial religion. It also changed social and political life. Jonathan Edwards of Massachusetts was one of the most important leaders of the time. His dramatic sermons told sinners to ask forgiveness for their sins or face punishment in hell forever.

In 1738 British minister George Whitefield made the first of seven trips to America. He held revivals from Georgia to New England. Ministers like Whitefield emphasized personal religious experiences over church doctrine.

STANDARDS PRACTICE

DIRECTIONS Read each question and circle the letter of the best response.

1 What was the Great Awakening?

A another name for the Enlightenment

B another name for the Age of Reason

C a political movement that swept through the American colonies

D a religious movement that swept through the American colonies

2 In what way were revivals revolutionary?

A Religious leaders were trying to take over the government.

B They advocated the violent overthrow of all governments.

C They emphasized personal experience over church doctrine.

D They encouraged people to break laws that conflict with their religious beliefs.

STANDARDS REVIEW

The Great Awakening drew people from different regions, classes, and races. Ministers allowed ordinary church members to play a role in services, no matter what their race, class, or gender. Women, African Americans, Native Americans, and poor people often took part in services. The value placed on each individual helped shape American political ideas about who should have a say in government.

The Great Awakening raised ideas that had an effect on colonial politics. Sermons about spiritual equality of all people led some colonists to begin asking for more political equality. Revivals became popular places to talk about political and social issues. Ministers from different colonies began sharing ideas with one another. People from colonies where there was less political freedom were introduced to more democratic systems used in other colonies.

STANDARDS PRACTICE

DIRECTIONS Read each question and circle the letter of the best response.

3 How did revivals help shape American political ideas about who should have a say in government?

A by placing value on individuals of all types

B by preaching that anyone could go to heaven

C by allowing women to be ordained as ministers

D by condemning the institution of slavery

4 How did the ideas raised in the Great Awakening affect American politics?

A Sermons about spiritual equality led colonists to begin asking for more political equality.

B Revivals were popular places to talk about political and social issues.

C People from colonies where there was less political freedom were introduced to more democratic systems used in other colonies.

D all of the above

Name ______________________ Class ______________ Date ______________

STANDARDS REVIEW

HSS 8.1 Students understand the major events preceding the founding of the nation and relate their significance to the development of American constitutional democracy.

8.1.2 Analyze the philosophy of government expressed in the Declaration of Independence, with an emphasis on government as a means of securing individual rights (e.g., key phrases such as "all men are created equal, that they are endowed by their Creator with certain unalienable Rights").

> We hold these truths to be self-evident, that all men are created equal, that they are endowed by their Creator with certain unalienable Rights, that among these are Life, Liberty, and the pursuit of Happiness. That to secure these rights, Governments are instituted among Men, deriving their just powers from the consent of the governed, That whenever any Form of Government becomes destructive of these ends, it is the Right of the People to alter or to abolish it, and to institute new Government, laying its foundations on such principles and organizing its powers in such form, as to them shall seem most likely to effect their Safety and Happiness.
>
> from *The Declaration of Independence*

In June 1776 the Second Continental Congress created a committee to write a document declaring the colonies' independence. The committee members included John Adams, Benjamin Franklin, and Thomas Jefferson. Jefferson was the main author of the document.

STANDARDS PRACTICE

DIRECTIONS Read each question and circle the letter of the best response.

1 Who was the main author of the Declaration of Independence?

A John Adams
B Benjamin Franklin
C Thomas Jefferson
D George Washington

2 According to the Declaration of Independence, where does the power of government come from?

A the Creator
B Congress
C Thomas Jefferson
D the consent of the governed

STANDARDS REVIEW

The Declaration of Independence formally announced the colonies' break from Great Britain. It also expressed three main ideas. The first idea was that all men possess unalienable rights. These basic rights include "life, liberty, and the pursuit of happiness."

The second idea, or argument, was that King George III had violated the colonists' rights violations. There is a list of over 25 rights' violations. For example, Jefferson charged the king with passing unfair laws and interfering with colonial governments. Jefferson also accused the king of taxing colonists without their consent. The presence of a large British army in the colonies was seen as another violation of colonists' rights.

Third, Jefferson argued that the colonies had the right to break away from Great Britain and form a new government. Jefferson was influenced by the Enlightenment idea of the social contract. This is the idea that governments and rulers must protect the rights of citizens. In exchange, the people agree to be governed. Jefferson said that because King George III had broken the social contract with the colonists, the colonists should no longer obey him.

On July 4, 1776, the Continental Congress approved the Declaration of Independence. This act broke all ties to the British Crown. The United States of America was born.

STANDARDS PRACTICE

DIRECTIONS Read each question and circle the letter of the best response.

3 According to the Declaration of Independence, what unalienable rights do all men possess?

- **A** liberty, equality, and fraternity
- **B** life, liberty, and the pursuit of happiness
- **C** equal rights
- **D** civil rights

4 Who does the Declaration of Independence accuse of having broken the social contract?

- **A** King George III
- **B** John Adams
- **C** Benjamin Franklin
- **D** Thomas Jefferson

STANDARDS REVIEW

HSS 8.1 Students understand the major events preceding the founding of the nation and relate their significance to the development of American constitutional democracy.

8.1.3 Analyze how the American Revolution affected other nations, especially France.

After the Battle of Saratoga, France and Spain offered help to the American Patriots. Both countries were powerful enemies of Great Britain. The American Revolution also inspired individuals from other countries to help the Patriots' cause.

Bernardo de Gálvez, the governor of Spanish Louisiana, led a small army that seized British ports from Louisiana all the way to Pensacola, Florida. Among the ports seized by the Spanish was the British stronghold of Fort Charlotte at present-day Mobile, Alabama.

The Marquis de Lafayette, a French nobleman, was devoted to human freedom. Although he spoke little English, had never seen battle, and was not yet 20 years old, he enlisted in the Continental Army without pay. He became a skilled military officer. In addition, he contributed $200,000 of his own money to support the revolution and helped persuade France to send more aid to the Americans.

Another European officer, Baron Friedrich von Steuben, brought a lifetime of military experience from his homeland of Prussia, in modern-day Germany. Under his training, the Continental Army became a tough fighting force.

STANDARDS PRACTICE

DIRECTIONS Read each question and circle the letter of the best response.

1 What event led the French and Spanish to offer their help to the American Patriots?

A the signing of the Declaration of Independence
B the Battle of Bunker Hill
C the Battle of Saratoga
D the seizure of British ports

2 How did the Marquis de Lafayette help the American cause?

A as a skilled military officer
B by contributing money
C by helping persuade France to send aid to the Americans
D all of the above

STANDARDS REVIEW

In 1789 the French people overthrew their king and replaced the monarchy with a republican form of government. Many French citizens were inspired by the American Revolution. Many Americans thought that France was creating the same kind of democracy as the United States. Others were not so pleased. They worried about the French Revolution's attacks on traditional authority. Many Americans were shocked when the French king and queen were beheaded in 1793.

A few months after the beginning of the French Revolution, war broke out between France and Great Britain. Some Americans supported the French, while others supported the British. In 1793 a Neutrality Proclamation stated that the United States would not take sides with any European countries that were at war.

President George Washington believed that this plan of neutrality was the safest and most reasonable, but not everyone agreed. Thomas Jefferson wanted the French revolutionaries to succeed. He believed that the United States should back France because France had supported the United States during the Revolutionary War. On the other hand, Alexander Hamilton was pro-British. He wanted to strengthen trading ties with Britain, which was the most powerful trading nation in the world.

STANDARDS PRACTICE

DIRECTIONS Read each question and circle the letter of the best response.

3 What event helped inspire the French Revolution?

A war with Great Britain
B the beheading of the French king and queen
C the American Revolution
D the Neutrality Proclamation

4 What did the Neutrality Proclamation state?

A that the United States would never go to war
B that the United States would not take sides with any European countries that were at war
C that the United States would support France
D that the United States would support Great Britain

STANDARDS REVIEW

HSS 8.1 Students understand the major events preceding the founding of the nation and relate their significance to the development of American constitutional democracy.

8.1.4 Describe the nation's blend of civic republicanism, classical liberal principles, and English parliamentary traditions.

In forming a new government, the American people drew from a wide range of political ideas. One of these was English law. England had limited the power of its kings and queens in two documents. These were the Magna Carta and the English Bill of Rights. The Magna Carta, signed by King John in 1215, required the king or queen to follow the same laws as other English people. The English Bill of Rights was passed in 1689. It prevented the king or queen from passing new taxes or changing laws without Parliament's approval.

Americans were also influenced by the liberal principles of the Enlightenment. The ideas of one Enlightenment philosopher, John Locke, were especially popular in America. Locke believed that there was a social contract between political leaders and the people they ruled. Under this contract, the government had a duty to protect people's rights. Americans also looked to the ideas of the French philosopher Baron de Montesquieu. He believed that the only way people could achieve liberty was through the separation of governmental powers.

STANDARDS PRACTICE

DIRECTIONS Read each question and circle the letter of the best response.

1 Why is the Magna Carta important?

A It keeps the king or queen from passing new taxes.
B It requires the king or queen to obey the law.
C It is a social contract.
D It provides for the separation of governmental powers.

2 According to John Locke, government exists for which of the following reasons?

A to civilize people
B to rule people
C to wage war
D to protect people's rights

STANDARDS REVIEW

Americans had also developed their own models of self-government. In New England, colonists held town meetings where they elected their officials. In Virginia, the House of Burgesses was the first elected assembly in any British colony. In addition, in 1620 the Pilgrims had signed the Mayflower Compact to govern themselves at Plymouth colony.

In 1639, the people of Connecticut had drawn up a plan of government called the Fundamental Orders of Connecticut. This is considered to be the first written constitution in the English colonies. Finally, the Declaration of Independence set forth the beliefs on which Americans thought government should be based.

During the American Revolution nearly every colony wrote a new state constitution. These constitutions supported republicanism. In a republic, citizens elect representatives to represent them and these elected officials are responsible to the people.

To keep individual leaders from gaining too much power, state constitutions also created limited governments. These are governments in which all leaders have to obey the laws and no one has total power.

Most state constitutions had rules to protect the rights of citizens. Some banned slavery. Some protected individual rights. For example, the Virginia Declaration of Rights defended the rights of a trial by jury, freedom of the press, and ownership of property.

STANDARDS PRACTICE

DIRECTIONS Read each question and circle the letter of the best response.

3 What was the first written constitution in the English colonies?

- **A** the Fundamental Orders of Connecticut
- **B** the Mayflower Compact
- **C** the Declaration of Independence
- **D** the Virginia Declaration of Rights

4 How does a republic function?

- **A** The people hold meetings where they pass their own laws.
- **B** Citizens elect representatives who are responsible to the people.
- **C** It is ruled by a council appointed by the ruler.
- **D** Hired lawmakers are required to sign a social contract.

STANDARDS REVIEW

HSS 8.2 Students analyze the political principles underlying the U.S. Constitution and compare the enumerated and implied powers of the federal government.

8.2.1 Discuss the significance of the Magna Carta, the English Bill of Rights, and the Mayflower Compact.

One source of inspiration for the newly independent American government was English law. England had limited the power of its kings and queens in two documents. These were the Magna Carta and the English Bill of Rights. The Magna Carta was signed by King John in 1215. It required the king to follow the same laws as other English people.

The English Bill of Rights was passed in 1689. It reduced the power of the English monarch. At the same time, Parliament gained power. The king or queen was prohibited from passing new taxes or changing laws without Parliament's approval. As a result, the people's representatives had a strong voice in government.

The American colonists were greatly interested in this shift in power from monarchs to a representative governing body. As time went on, the colonists valued their own right to elect representatives to decide local issues. Following these changes, the colonies quickly formed new assemblies and charters. The Virginia House of Burgesses was the first elected assembly established in any British colony.

STANDARDS PRACTICE

DIRECTIONS Read each question and circle the letter of the best response.

1 What document gave the English Parliament more power?

A the Magna Carta
B the English Bill of Rights
C the Mayflower Compact
D the Constitution

2 How did the American colonists react to the shift of power from the monarch to Parliament?

A by declaring war
B by declaring independence
C by forming new assemblies and charters
D by overthrowing the king

STANDARDS REVIEW

> We whose names are underwritten, . . . having undertaken, for the glory of God, and advancement of the Christian faith, and the honour of our King and country, a voyage to plant the first colony in the northern parts of Virginia, do by these presents solemnly and mutually in the presence of God, and one of another, covenant and combine ourselves into a civil body politic for our better ordering and preservation and furtherance of the ends aforesaid; and by virtue hereof, to enact, constitute, and frame such just and equal laws, ordinances, acts, constitutions, and offices . . . as shall be thought most meet and convenient for the general good of the colony until which we promise all due . . . obedience.
>
> from *The Mayflower Compact*

In 1620, the Pilgrim leaders aboard the *Mayflower* signed the Mayflower Compact to govern themselves at Plymouth Colony. A compact is a legal contract. In it, they agreed to make "just and equal laws . . . for the general good of the colony." This was one of the first attempts at self-government in the English colonies.

Americans had other models of self-government to refer to. In New England, colonists held town meetings where they elected their officials. In 1639 the people of Connecticut drew up a plan of government called the Fundamental Orders of Connecticut. This document is considered to be the first written constitution in the English colonies.

STANDARDS PRACTICE

DIRECTIONS Read each question and circle the letter of the best response.

3 What reasons did the Mayflower leaders give for planting a new colony?

A to glorify God
B to advance Christianity
C to honor the king
D all of the above

4 According to the Mayflower Compact, who would benefit from any laws enacted under its terms?

A the general population
B the leaders
C the captain of the ship
D the king of England

History–Social Science Grade 8 — Standard 8.2.2

STANDARDS REVIEW

HSS 8.2 Students analyze the political principles underlying the U.S. Constitution and compare the enumerated and implied powers of the federal government.

8.2.2 Analyze the Articles of Confederation and the Constitution and the success of each in implementing the ideals of the Declaration of Independence.

Under the Articles of Confederation, there was one branch of national government, the Confederation Congress, but it had limited powers. By limiting the powers of the national government, the drafters hoped to protect the liberties of the people. Each state had one vote in the Congress. States had the power to refuse requests from Congress. Also, there was no president or national court system.

Under the Articles of Confederation, Congress could not force states to provide soldiers for an army. It could do little to enforce international treaties. Congress did not have the authority to pass tariffs or to order the states to pass tariffs. Nor did the Confederation Congress have any power to regulate trade between the states. Some states printed worthless money to pay their war debts. Massachusetts tried to pay its war debts by collecting taxes on land, leading to a rebellion.

The weakness of the Confederation government soon led some Americans to admit that the Articles of Confederation had failed to protect the ideas of liberty set forth in the Declaration of Independence.

STANDARDS PRACTICE

DIRECTIONS Read each question and circle the letter of the best response.

1 Which of the following best describes the government created by the Articles of Confederation?

- **A** It consisted of a single branch.
- **B** There was a strong Congress.
- **C** The president had more power than Congress.
- **D** Each state had a vote in Congress based on its population.

2 Why was the government created by the Articles of Confederation doomed to failure?

- **A** Congress could not force states to provide soldiers for an army.
- **B** Congress could not pass tariffs.
- **C** States printed worthless money to pay their war debts.
- **D** all of the above

STANDARDS REVIEW

The Constitution provides a structure for governing the United States. It divides powers between the states and the federal government. Some powers, such as the coining of money, the regulation of interstate and international trade, defense, and diplomacy, are delegated to the federal government.

Other powers are kept by the state governments or the citizens. They include creating local governments and holding elections. States also control education and trade within their borders.

Some powers are shared by the federal and state governments. These include taxation, borrowing money, enforcing laws, and providing for citizens' welfare.

The Constitution created three branches of government, executive, judicial, and legislative, that share power. It also created a system of checks and balances to keep any of the three branches of government from becoming too powerful.

In order to ensure the passage of the Constitution, a Bill of Rights was promised. The first 10 amendments to the Constitution guarantee the basic rights of all citizens. Without these safeguards, a person's rights would not always be protected because, under majority rule, the greatest number of people can make policies for everyone. The Bill of Rights guarantees such basic human rights as freedom of religion, freedom of the press, freedom of speech, freedom of assembly, and the right to petition.

STANDARDS PRACTICE

DIRECTIONS Read each question and circle the letter of the best response.

3 Which of the following powers does the Constitution delegate to the federal government alone?

A taxation
B holding elections
C coining of money
D enforcing laws

4 How did the framers of the Constitution guarantee the basic rights of all citizens?

A They divided powers between the federal and state governments.
B They created three branches of government.
C They added a Bill of Rights.
D They created a system of checks and balances.

STANDARDS REVIEW

HSS 8.2 Students analyze the political principles underlying the U.S. Constitution and compare the enumerated and implied powers of the federal government.

8.2.3 Evaluate the major debates that occurred during the development of the Constitution and their ultimate resolutions in such areas as shared power among institutions, divided state-federal power, slavery, the rights of individuals and states (later addressed by the addition of the Bill of Rights), and the status of American Indian nations under the commerce clause.

Some members of the Constitutional Convention wanted only small changes to the Articles of Confederation, while others wanted to rewrite the Articles completely. Most of the delegates at the Constitutional Convention wanted a strong national government. At the same time, they wanted to protect the idea that political authority belongs to the people. Delegates also wanted to balance the power of the national government with the powers of the states. They did this through federalism, sharing power between a central government and the states that make up a nation. The drafted Constitution gives states control over all government functions not specifically assigned to the federal government, such as control of local government and education. States also have the power to create and oversee civil and criminal law. Finally, states must protect the welfare of their citizens.

STANDARDS PRACTICE

DIRECTIONS Read each question and circle the letter of the best response.

1 Under the Constitution, who does political authority belong to?

A the people
B the federal government
C the state governments
D It is shared by the federal and state governments.

2 What powers does the Constitution give to the states?

A the power to create and oversee civil and criminal law
B the power to protect the welfare of their citizens
C control over government functions not specifically assigned to the federal government
D all of the above

STANDARDS REVIEW

Delegates from Virginia wanted a legislature with two chambers made up of representatives chosen on the basis of population. An alternate plan proposed by New Jersey delegates called for a single chamber in which each state would have an equal number of votes.

Southern states wanted slaves to be counted as part of their state populations, which would give them more representatives, and thus more power, in Congress. Northerners disagreed. They wanted the number of slaves to determine taxes but not representation. A compromise was reached. Three-fifths of the slaves were included as part of that state's population. Some delegates wanted to ban foreign slave trade completely. Many southern delegates threatened to leave the Union if the Constitution immediately ended the slave trade. Another compromise was made. Northern delegates agreed to stop asking that the slave trade be banned, and southern delegates agreed to stop requiring a two-thirds majority vote for laws to be passed in Congress. The words *slavery* and *slave* were left out of the Constitution.

The Commerce Clause gives Congress the power to "regulate commerce with … the Indian Tribes." This has been interpreted to mean that the states cannot tax or interfere with business on Indian reservations, but the federal government can. It allows Native American groups to develop their own governments and laws. These laws can be challenged in federal court. Reservation lands usually belong to the governments of Native American groups, but they are administered by the U.S. government.

STANDARDS PRACTICE

DIRECTIONS Read each question and circle the letter of the best response.

3 How did the Constitution count slaves to decide representation?

- **A** Each slave was counted as part of a state's population.
- **B** Because they were not citizens, slaves were not counted.
- **C** Three-fifths were counted.
- **D** none of the above

4 Who has the power to regulate commerce with Native American tribes?

- **A** Congress
- **B** the Interstate Commerce Commission
- **C** reservation officials appointed by the president
- **D** a council made up of elected representatives of the tribes

Name ______________________ Class ____________ Date ____________

History–Social Science Grade 8

Standard 8.2.4

STANDARDS REVIEW

HSS 8.2 Students analyze the political principles underlying the U.S. Constitution and compare the enumerated and implied powers of the federal government.

8.2.4 Describe the political philosophy underpinning the Constitution as specified in the *Federalist Papers* (authored by James Madison, Alexander Hamilton, and John Jay) and the role of such leaders as Madison, George Washington, Roger Sherman, Gouverneur Morris, and James Wilson in the writing and ratification of the Constitution.

One of the most important defenses of the proposed Constitution appeared in a series of essays that became known as the *Federalist Papers.* They were published anonymously, but historians now know that they were written by Alexander Hamilton, James Madison, and John Jay.

The authors of the *Federalist Papers* reassured Americans that the new federal government would not overpower the states. In one essay, Madison argued that the diversity of the United States would prevent any single group from dominating the government. The *Federalist Papers* were widely reprinted as the debate over the Constitution continued. In addition, George Washington and Benjamin Franklin endorsed the Constitution, winning additional support.

Washington had served as president of the Constitutional Convention, while Franklin had been the oldest delegate. Several important leaders did not attend the convention. John Adams and Thomas Jefferson were serving as ambassadors. Patrick Henry did not attend because he did not believe in a stronger central government.

STANDARDS PRACTICE

DIRECTIONS Read each question and circle the letter of the best response.

1 Which of the following was an author of the Federalist Papers?

A John Adams
B Benjamin Franklin
C Alexander Hamilton
D Thomas Jefferson

2 Who served as president of the Constitutional Convention?

A Alexander Hamilton
B Patrick Henry
C James Madison
D George Washington

STANDARDS REVIEW

James Madison wrote most of the Virginia Plan for the Constitution, which called for a new federal constitution that would give supreme power to the central government. It allowed for three branches of national government—the executive, judicial, and legislative branches. Madison became known as the "Father of the Constitution" for his ideas about government. Under the Virginia Plan, there would be a legislature made up of two chambers. The chambers would be made up of representatives chosen on the basis of state population.

New Jersey delegate William Paterson presented the small-state or New Jersey Plan. It called for a one-house legislature in which each state would have an equal number of votes, and thus an equal voice, in the federal government. This plan also gave the federal government the right to tax citizens in all states and to regulate commerce.

Roger Sherman presented the Great Compromise, which led to the signing of the Constitution. Each state, regardless of size, would have an equal voice in the upper house of the legislature. In the lower house, each state would have a number of representatives based on the state's population.

Gouverneur Morris of New York spoke out against the slave trade. The idea of banning the foreign slave trade prompted southerners such as John Rutledge of South Carolina to defend the practice. A compromise was finally reached, and the words *slavery* and *slave* were left out of the Constitution, which refers instead to "free Persons" and "all other persons."

STANDARDS PRACTICE

DIRECTIONS Read each question and circle the letter of the best response.

3 Who wrote down the ideas about government that formed the basis for the Constitution?

A Alexander Hamilton
B Thomas Jefferson
C James Madison
D Roger Sherman

4 Under the Great Compromise, which house of Congress follows the New Jersey Plan?

A the lower house
B the upper house
C both houses
D neither house

STANDARDS REVIEW

HSS 8.2 Students analyze the political principles underlying the U.S. Constitution and compare the enumerated and implied powers of the federal government.

8.2.5 Understand the significance of Jefferson's Statute for Religious Freedom as a forerunner of the First Amendment and the origins, purpose, and differing views of the founding fathers on the issue of the separation of church and state.

Thomas Jefferson's ideas about religious freedom were included in the Virginia Statute for Religious Freedom. This document declared that no person could be forced to attend a particular church or be required to pay for a church with tax money.

The Virginia Statute for Religious Freedom served as the basis for the beginning of the First Amendment. It begins, "Congress shall make no law respecting an establishment of religion, or prohibiting the free exercise thereof." In other words, the government cannot support or interfere with the practice of a religion. This amendment keeps the government from favoring one religion over any other. When the Constitution was written, many countries had an official state religion.

By 1833 no state within the United States had an "official" church.

STANDARDS PRACTICE

DIRECTIONS Read each question and circle the letter of the best response.

1 What document served as the basis for the beginning of the First Amendment?

A the Virginia Declaration of Rights
B the Virginia Statute for Religious Freedom
C the Declaration of Independence
D the English Bill of Rights

2 What is the purpose of the beginning of the First Amendment?

A It requires all citizens to practice a religion.
B It establishes an official state religion.
C It keeps the government from favoring one religion over another.
D It allows the government to support religious institutions.

STANDARDS REVIEW

> II. Be it enacted by the General assembly, that no man shall be compelled to frequent or support any religious worship, place, or ministry whatsoever, nor shall be enforced, restrained, molested, or burthened in his body or goods, not shall otherwise suffer on account of his religious opinions or belief; but that all men shall be free to profess, and by argument to maintain, their opinion in matters of religion, that that the same shall in no wise diminish, enlarge, or affect their civil capacities.
>
> III. And though we well know that this assembly elected by the people for the ordinary purposes of legislation only, have no power to restrain the acts of succeeding assemblies, constituted with powers equal to our own, and that therefore to declare this act to be irrevocable would be of no effect in law; yet we are free to declare, and do declare, that the rights hereby asserted are of the natural rights of mankind, and that if any act shall be hereafter passed to repeal the present, or to narrow its operation, such act will be an infringement of natural right.
>
> from *the Virginia Statute for Religious Freedom*

STANDARDS PRACTICE

DIRECTIONS Read each question and circle the letter of the best response.

3 Which of the following is true of the Virginia Statute for Religious Freedom?

A People cannot be forced to attend or support any religious worship.
B People cannot be discriminated against on account of their religious beliefs.
C People must be allowed to have their own opinions about religion.
D all of the above

4 According to paragraph III above, what kind of right is freedom of religion?

A a civil right
B a human right
C a natural right
D a God-given right

5 What possibility did Jefferson foresee in Paragraph III?

A that the statute might be revoked in the future
B that the statute would become national law
C that the statute would become part of the Constitution
D that religion would be outlawed

History–Social Science Grade 8 — Standard 8.2.6

STANDARDS REVIEW

HSS 8.2 Students analyze the political principles underlying the U.S. Constitution and compare the enumerated and implied powers of the federal government.

8.2.6 Enumerate the powers of government set forth in the Constitution and the fundamental liberties ensured by the Bill of Rights.

The United States is a representative democracy. This means that the government is led by officials chosen by the people. The Constitution divides powers between the states and the federal government.

Delegated powers are those powers granted by the Constitution to the federal government. They include the coining of money and the regulation of interstate and international trade. The federal government also runs the country's defense, declares war, and conducts diplomacy.

Reserved powers are those powers kept by the state governments or the citizens. They include creating local governments and holding elections. States also control education and trade within their borders.

Concurrent powers are those powers shared by the federal and state governments. These include taxation, borrowing money, enforcing laws, and providing for citizens' welfare.

When "necessary and proper," Congress has the authority to stretch its delegated powers to deal with new or unexpected issues. The elastic clause is found in Article I, Section 8 of the Constitution. It provides flexibility for the government.

STANDARDS PRACTICE

DIRECTIONS Read each question and circle the letter of the best response.

1 Powers that are granted by the Constitution to the federal government are

A concurrent powers.
B delegated powers.
C reserved powers.
D Constitutional powers.

2 What provision does the Constitution make for dealing with unexpected issues?

A the Bill of Rights
B the balance of powers
C the elastic clause
D concurrent powers

STANDARDS REVIEW

The Bill of Rights ensures that the rights of all citizens are protected. The ideas spelled out in the First Amendment form the most basic rights of all U.S. citizens. These rights include freedom of religion, freedom of the press, freedom of speech, freedom of assembly, and the right to petition.

The Second Amendment deals with state militias and the right to bear arms. The Third Amendment prevents the military from forcing citizens to house soldiers. The Fourth Amendment prohibits "unreasonable searches and seizures."

The next four amendments provide guidelines for trying people accused of crimes. Under the Fifth Amendment, the government cannot punish anyone without due process of law. The Sixth Amendment guarantees the right to a speedy public trial by jury and the right of the accused to have an attorney defend them. The Seventh Amendment allows juries to decide civil cases. The Eighth Amendment bans excessive bail, excessive fines, and cruel and unusual punishment.

The Ninth Amendment says that the rights listed in the Constitution are not the only rights that citizens have. Under the Tenth Amendment any powers that the Constitution does not specifically give to Congress or prohibit to the states belong to the states and to the people. Thus, it protects citizens' rights. It helps to keep the balance of power between the federal and state governments.

STANDARDS PRACTICE

DIRECTIONS Read each question and circle the letter of the best response.

3 Which of the following rights is not guaranteed by the First Amendment?

A freedom of religion
B freedom of speech
C the right to bear arms
D the right to petition

4 Which amendment guarantees that no one can be punished without due process of law?

A the First Amendment
B the Second Amendment
C the Fourth Amendment
D the Fifth Amendment

Name ______________________ Class ______________ Date ______________

History–Social Science Grade 8 — Standard 8.2.7

STANDARDS REVIEW

HSS 8.2 Students analyze the political principles underlying the U.S. Constitution and compare the enumerated and implied powers of the federal government.

8.2.7 Describe the principles of federalism, dual sovereignty, separation of powers, checks and balances, the nature and purpose of majority rule, and the ways in which the American idea of constitutionalism preserves individual rights.

The Constitution provides a structure for governing the United States. It divides powers between the states and the federal government. Some powers are shared by the federal and state governments. These include taxation, borrowing money, enforcing laws, and providing for citizens' welfare. This sharing of power is known as federalism.

Before the Civil War, federalism was closely related to dual sovereignty. Dual sovereignty is the idea that the federal government and the states each had exclusive power over their own spheres.

The Constitution provides for three branches of government—legislative, executive, and judicial. This separation of powers is enforced by a system of checks and balances to keep any of the three branches of government from becoming too powerful.

For example, the legislative branch has the power to propose and pass bills into law. The executive branch has the power to veto, or reject, the laws that Congress passes. However, Congress can override a veto. The judicial branch has the power to review laws passed by Congress and strike down any law that violates the Constitution.

STANDARDS PRACTICE

DIRECTIONS Read each question and circle the letter of the best response.

1 What concept was closely related to dual sovereignty?

A federalism
B balance of powers
C the power to veto
D checks and balances

2 Why is a system of checks and balances necessary?

A to make laws
B to enforce laws
C to keep any of the three branches of the government from becoming too powerful
D to ensure that the three branches of government work together

STANDARDS REVIEW

A Congress consisting of a Senate and a House of Representatives forms the legislative branch. Congress has the power to collect taxes, to borrow money, to regulate commerce with foreign countries and among the states, to coin money, to establish post offices, to declare war, to raise and support military forces, and to make any laws necessary to carry out any of the specified powers.

The executive branch is made up of the president and vice president. The president is commander in chief of the armed forces. The president also has the right to make treaties and appointments, with the approval of the Senate. The judicial branch of the government consists of federal courts and judges, including the Supreme Court.

Article V of the Constitution provides a way to change the document when necessary to reflect the will of the people. Amendments must be approved by a two-thirds majority of each house of Congress and by three-fourths of the states.

The first 10 amendments to the Constitution are known as the Bill of Rights. They guarantee the basic rights of all citizens. Without these safeguards, individual rights would not always be protected under majority rule. Under majority rule, the greatest number of people can make policies for everyone. The First Amendment guarantees freedom of religion, freedom of the press, freedom of speech, freedom of assembly, and the right to petition.

STANDARDS PRACTICE

DIRECTIONS Read each question and circle the letter of the best response.

3 Under the Constitution, who has the power to declare war?

A the president
B the Supreme Court
C Congress
D the states

4 If the Constitution guarantees majority rule, why is a Bill of Rights necessary?

A to protect the rights of the majority
B to protect the rights of individuals
C to allow the Constitution to be changed by adding amendments
D It wasn't necessary.

Name ______________________ Class ____________ Date ____________

History–Social Science Grade 8 — Standard 8.3.1

STANDARDS REVIEW

HSS 8.3 Students understand the foundation of the American political system and the ways in which citizens participate in it.

8.3.1 Analyze the principles and concepts codified in state constitutions between 1777 and 1781 that created the context out of which American political institutions and ideas developed.

During the American Revolution nearly every colony wrote a new state constitution. These constitutions supported republicanism. In a republic, citizens elect representatives who are responsible to the people.

To keep individual leaders from gaining too much power, state constitutions also created limited governments. These are governments in which all leaders have to obey the laws and no one has total power.

Most state constitutions had rules to protect the rights of citizens. Some banned slavery. Some protected individual rights. For example, the Virginia Declaration of Rights defended the rights of a trial by jury, freedom of the press, and ownership of property. The Virginia Statute for Religious Freedom declared that no person could be forced to attend a particular church or be required to pay for a church with tax money.

Many states' constitutions expanded voting rights by allowing any white man who paid taxes to vote. Some states granted suffrage only to white men who owned property. In most states only property owners could hold elected office. Seven state constitutions gave suffrage to free African American men. However, by the 1860s these rights were taken away or greatly limited. New Jersey, the only state to allow American women to vote, revoked this right in 1807.

STANDARDS PRACTICE

DIRECTIONS Read each question and circle the letter of the best response.

1 What form of government was supported by early state constitutions?

A republicanism
B direct rule
C indirect rule
D absolute rule

2 Under most early state constitutions, who could hold elected office?

A any man or woman
B any white man or woman
C property owners
D any voter

STANDARDS REVIEW

HSS 8.3 Students understand the foundation of the American political system and the ways in which citizens participate in it.

8.3.2 Explain how the ordinances of 1785 and 1787 privatized national resources and transferred federally owned lands into private holdings, townships, and states.

After the American Revolution, Congress had to decide what to do with the western lands now under its control. It also had to raise money to pay national debts. It tried to solve both problems by selling the western lands to the public. In May 1785 Congress passed the Land Ordinance of 1785. It set up a system for surveying and dividing the public territory. The land was split into townships of 36 square miles. Each township was divided into 36 lots of 640 acres each. One lot was saved for a school, and four for Revolutionary War veterans. The rest of the lots were sold.

To create a political system for the region, Congress passed the Northwest Ordinance of 1787. It established the Northwest Territory, which included the area that is now Illinois, Indiana, Michigan, Ohio, and Wisconsin. The Ordinance of 1787 set up a system for dividing the Northwest Territory into several smaller territories. When the population of a territory reached 60,000, its settlers could draft a constitution and ask Congress for permission to join the Union as a state. The ordinance had a bill of rights to protect civil liberties. It made public education a basic right. It also outlawed slavery in the territory.

STANDARDS PRACTICE

DIRECTIONS Read each question and circle the letter of the best response.

1 How large was a township?

A 640 square miles
B 36 square miles
C 640 acres
D 36 acres

2 Which of the following was made a basic right under the Northwest Ordinance of 1787?

A the right to bear arms
B the right to vote
C freedom of religion
D public education

STANDARDS REVIEW

HSS 8.3 Students understand the foundation of the American political system and the ways in which citizens participate in it.

8.3.3 Enumerate the advantages of a common market among the states as foreseen in and protected by the Constitution's clauses on interstate commerce, common coinage, and full-faith and credit.

Under the Articles of Confederation, Congress had no power to regulate interstate commerce. States followed their own trade interests, and trade laws differed from state to state. This made trade difficult for merchants whose businesses crossed state lines. States could also print their own paper money. The result was the beginnings of inflation. This money often was worthless because states did not have the gold or silver to back it up. Additionally, Congress had no power to stop states from issuing more paper money.

The Constitution sought to rectify these problems. Article I, Section 8, gives the federal government the right to pass tariffs, regulate international trade and interstate commerce, and to coin money. Article I, Section 10, specifically prohibits the states from coining money or passing tariffs. Article IV, Section 1, states that "Full Faith and Credit shall be given in each State to the public Acts, Records, and judicial Proceedings of every other State." In other words, each state is required to respect the laws of other states.

STANDARDS PRACTICE

DIRECTIONS Read each question and circle the letter of the best response.

1 Under the Articles of Confederation, trade between states was difficult

A because they used the same money.

B because trade laws differed from one state to another.

C because people in different states did not speak the same language.

D because there were no interstate highways.

2 What does the "full-faith and credit" clause of the Constitution mean?

A Each state must give credit to other states for interstate trade.

B Each state must allow its citizens to follow the faith of their choice.

C Each state must respect the laws of other states.

D Each state must respect the U.S. Constitution.

STANDARDS REVIEW

HSS 8.3 Students understand the foundation of the American political system and the ways in which citizens participate in it.

8.3.4 Understand how the conflicts between Thomas Jefferson and Alexander Hamilton resulted in the emergence of two political parties (e.g., view of foreign policy, Alien and Sedition Acts, economic policy, National Bank, funding and assumption of the revolutionary debt).

Alexander Hamilton wanted the federal government to pay most of the Revolutionary War debt, which he thought would help the national economy. Southern states such as Virginia and North Carolina were opposed to this because they did not have many war debts. Hamilton also wanted to start a national bank. He wanted a strong federal government that supported industry and trade. Thomas Jefferson and James Madison wanted to limit the federal government's power and believed that a national bank would give it too much power.

After the French Revolution, Jefferson wanted the United States to back the new government in France because France had helped the United States during the Revolutionary War. Hamilton was pro-British. He hoped to strengthen trading ties with Britain.

In the summer of 1798 Federalists in Congress passed the Alien and Sedition Acts. The Alien Act allowed the president to remove foreign residents he thought were involved in plots against the government. The Sedition Act said U.S. citizens could not write, print, utter, or publish any false or hostile words against the government. Jefferson and Madison passed the Kentucky and Virginia Resolutions, which said the Alien and Sedition Acts were unconstitutional and could therefore be ignored by the states.

STANDARDS PRACTICE

DIRECTIONS Read each question and circle the letter of the best response.

1 Who wanted a national bank?

A Hamilton
B Jefferson
C Madison
D all of the above

2 Who was opposed to the Alien and Sedition Acts?

A Jefferson
B Madison
C both A and B
D none of the above

Name ______________________ Class ______________ Date ____________

History–Social Science Grade 8 — Standard 8.3.5

STANDARDS REVIEW

HSS 8.3 Students understand the foundation of the American political system and the ways in which citizens participate in it.

8.3.5 Know the significance of domestic resistance movements and ways in which the central government responded to such movements (e.g., Shays' Rebellion, the Whiskey Rebellion).

After the Revolutionary War, most states had a hard time paying off war debts. Massachusetts tried to pay its war debts by collecting taxes on land. This policy hit farmers hard. Many had trouble paying their debts, and the courts began to force them to sell their property. In September 1786, a poor farmer, Daniel Shays, led hundreds of men to shut down the Supreme Court in Springfield. His forces were defeated, and many of the rebels were imprisoned. Shays' Rebellion showed the weakness of the Confederation government. When Massachusetts asked the national government to help put down the rebellion, Congress could do little to help. Americans began to realize that they needed a stronger government that could protect the nation in times of crisis.

In March 1791, Congress passed a tax on American-made whiskey as part of Alexander Hamilton's plan to help pay the federal debt. Hamilton also wanted to test the power of the new federal government to control the states' actions. By 1794, farmers in western Pennsylvania had lashed out against the tax in what came to be known as the Whiskey Rebellion. President George Washington feared that the rebels threatened the federal government's authority. He personally led a militia against the rebellion in November 1794, but by that time most of the rebels had fled. The Whiskey Rebellion ended without a battle.

STANDARDS PRACTICE

DIRECTIONS Read each question and circle the letter of the best response.

1 How did Massachusetts try to pay its war debts?

A by collecting an income tax
B by collecting a tax on land
C by seizing farmland
D by selling state parks

2 Besides paying the federal debt, what did Hamilton hope to accomplish with the whiskey tax?

A reduce alcoholism
B help the whiskey industry
C test the power of the federal government
D strengthen the power of the states

STANDARDS REVIEW

HSS 8.3 Students understand the foundation of the American political system and the ways in which citizens participate in it.

8.3.6 Describe the basic law-making process and how the Constitution provides numerous opportunities for citizens to participate in the political process and to monitor and influence government (e.g., function of elections, political parties, interest groups).

Laws may be proposed or rejected by the executive branch of government (the president), but the legislative branch (Congress) makes the nation's laws. The judicial branch (Supreme Court) reviews laws to make sure that they are constitutional. If a law is found to be unconstitutional, Congress can try to re-pass it.

Citizens have many opportunities to participate in the political process. Perhaps the most vital duty of a citizen is to take part in elections. By doing so, citizens decide who will lead their government.

In addition to voting, Americans can campaign for candidates or issues. They can give money to candidates directly or through political action committees, which collect money for candidates who support certain issues. Citizens sometimes work with interest groups to take political action. Individuals can express their thoughts and opinions in letters to leaders, or they can attend city council meetings. Active political participation is an important duty for U.S. citizens.

STANDARDS PRACTICE

DIRECTIONS Read each question and circle the letter of the best response.

1 What happens if the Supreme Court finds a law to be unconstitutional?

A Nothing happens.
B The law cannot go into effect.
C Congress can try to re-pass it.
D The president can overrule the Supreme Court's decision.

2 What is the most important way in which citizens can decide who will lead their government?

A by taking part in elections
B by giving money to candidates
C by working with interest groups
D by writing letters to leaders

STANDARDS REVIEW

HSS 8.3 Students understand the foundation of the American political system and the ways in which citizens participate in it.
8.3.7 Understand the functions and responsibilities of a free press.

The First Amendment to the Constitution guarantees freedom of the press. This means that Americans have the right to express their own ideas and views and the right to hear the ideas and views of others. As former senator Margaret Chase Smith said, "The key to security is public information."

The case of John Peter Zenger, publisher of the *New York Weekly Journal,* shows why freedom of the press is important. Zenger published statements that were critical of New York's royal governor. Zenger was arrested for "seditious libel" and imprisoned. He was put on trial eight months later, in 1735. At the end of the trial, the jury found Zenger not guilty because the statements he printed were true.

The Constitution does not protect against libel. Libel is intentionally writing and publishing a lie that harms another person.

STANDARDS PRACTICE

DIRECTIONS Read each question and circle the letter of the best response.

1 What is the meaning of the phrase "freedom of the press"?

- **A** People who own a press can print anything they want to.
- **B** People have the right to publish anything they want to.
- **C** People have the right to express their own ideas and views.
- **D** People can say whatever they want as long as they do not criticize members of the government.

2 Which of the following would not be protected by the First Amendment?

- **A** libel
- **B** an article criticizing a member of the government
- **C** public information
- **D** ideas and views that differ from one's own

STANDARDS REVIEW

HSS 8.4 Students analyze the aspirations and ideals of the people of the new nation.

8.4.1 Describe the country's physical landscapes, political divisions, and territorial expansion during the terms of the first four presidents.

When George Washington took office in 1789, the United States consisted of 11 states along the Atlantic coast. It also included the land between the Appalachian Mountains and the Mississippi River and south of the Great Lakes. The territory north of the Ohio River was referred to as the Northwest Territory.

By the early 1800s, thousands of Americans were pouring across the Appalachians to settle in the area between the mountains and the Mississippi River. As the region's population grew, Kentucky, Tennessee, and Ohio were admitted to the Union. Settlers in these states depended upon the Mississippi River to move their products to eastern markets.

In 1803, President Thomas Jefferson bought the territory of Louisiana from France for $15 million. It included the important port city of New Orleans at the mouth of the Mississippi River, and land between the Mississippi and the Rocky Mountains, including the Missouri River. The Louisiana Purchase almost doubled the size of the United States.

Oregon Country, in the Pacific Northwest, was claimed by the United States, Britain, Russia, and Spain.

STANDARDS PRACTICE

DIRECTIONS Read each question and circle the letter of the best response.

1 Where was the Northwest Territory?

A in the Pacific Northwest

B between the Mississippi River and the Rocky Mountains

C between the Ohio River and the Great Lakes

D between the Appalachians and the Mississippi River

2 Which of the following did not claim the Oregon Country?

A Britain

B France

C Russia

D Spain

STANDARDS REVIEW

HSS 8.4 Students analyze the aspirations and ideals of the people of the new nation.

8.4.2 Explain the policy significance of famous speeches (e.g., Washington's Farewell Address, Jefferson's 1801 Inaugural Address, John Q. Adams's Fourth of July 1821 Address).

In his Farewell Address, George Washington urged the United States to "steer clear" of permanent alliances with other nations, which he feared could draw the United States into war. He warned against the dangers of political parties, which he believed weakened government. He believed that political unity was a key to national success. He told the nation to work out its differences and protect its independence. He also thought the government should try to stay out of debt and not borrow money.

In his inaugural address, Thomas Jefferson stressed unity, saying "We are all Republicans, we are all Federalists." Jefferson wanted to make it clear that he supported the will of the majority. He stressed the need for a limited government and the protection of civil liberties. He wanted to keep government thrifty and taxes low so that they would not be a burden on working people.

In a speech before Congress on the Fourth of July, 1821, Secretary of State John Quincy Adams said that the United States had always been friendly with European powers. He said that the country did not want to be involved in wars with European countries. He implied that the United States supported the newly independent countries of Latin America, but would not fight their battles.

STANDARDS PRACTICE

DIRECTIONS Read each question and circle the letter of the best response.

1 Why was Washington opposed to political parties?

A He wanted to be dictator.

B He thought they were corrupt.

C He thought they weakened government.

D He wanted to stay in power.

2 According to Adams, what was the U.S. attitude toward the new nations of Latin America?

A The U.S. would help them fight.

B The U.S. would help the colonial rulers get them back.

C The U.S. wanted to rule them.

D The U.S. supported them but would not fight for them.

STANDARDS REVIEW

HSS 8.4 Students analyze the aspirations and ideals of the people of the new nation.

8.4.3 Analyze the rise of capitalism and the economic problems and conflicts that accompanied it (e.g., Jackson's opposition to the National Bank; early decisions of the U.S. Supreme Court that reinforced the sanctity of contracts and a capitalist economic system of law).

U.S. Representative Henry Clay proposed a series of measures intended to make the United States economically self-sufficient. He pushed for a protective tariff and a national bank to make interstate trade easier. Clay wanted tariff money to be used to improve roads and canals, which would help unite the country. Several Supreme Court rulings helped reinforce capitalism as the ruling economic system in the United States. In 1810 *Fletcher* v. *Peck* decreed that there was no difference between public and private contracts. In 1819 *Dartmouth College* v. *Woodward* placed contracts that were outside the control of state laws under control of the contract clause of the Constitution. In 1819 *McCulloch* v. *Maryland* found that states do not have the right to tax federal institutions. It also found that the national bank met the criteria of constitutionality. In 1824 *Gibbons* v *Ogden* decreed that only the federal government has the right to regulate interstate and foreign commerce.

President Andrew Jackson wanted to kill the national bank, and he moved most of its funds to state banks. In many cases, these banks used the funds to offer easy credit terms to people buying land, which helped expansion but led to inflation and, in 1837, to an economic depression.

STANDARDS PRACTICE

DIRECTIONS Read each question and circle the letter of the best response.

1 Which Supreme Court ruling found that the states do not have the right to tax federal institutions?

A *Fletcher* v. *Peck*
B *Dartmouth College* v. *Woodward*
C *McCulloch* v. *Maryland*
D *Gibbons* v. *Ogden*

2 What was the result of Jackson's moving funds from the national bank to state banks?

A an economic depression
B inflation
C More people bought land, which led to expansion.
D all of the above

History–Social Science Grade 8 Standard 8.4.4

STANDARDS REVIEW

HSS 8.4 Students analyze the aspirations and ideals of the people of the new nation.

8.4.4 Discuss daily life, including traditions in art, music, and literature, of early national America (e.g., through writings by Washington Irving, James Fenimore Cooper).

In 1790 the United States was home to almost four million people. Most Americans lived in the countryside and worked on farms. People in towns worked as craftspeople, laborers, or merchants. Cities were mostly small. Only New York City and Philadelphia had populations greater than 25,000.

Literature and art began to flourish. Washington Irving wrote humorous fiction. Irving warned Americans to learn from the past and be cautious of the future. He combined European influences with American settings and characters. James Fenimore Cooper wrote novels about the West and the Native Americans who lived on the frontier. His novel *The Last of the Mohicans* places fictional characters in a real historical setting. Artists began to paint landscapes that showed the history of America and the beauty of the land. By the 1830s the Hudson River School had emerged. It was a group of artists whose name came from the subject of many of their paintings. Their paintings reflected national pride and an appreciation of the American landscape.

During this time, people sang songs called spirituals. Spirituals are a type of folk hymn. Popular folk music of the period reflected the unique views of the growing nation in other ways. One of the most popular songs of the era, "Hunters of Kentucky," celebrated the Battle of New Orleans.

STANDARDS PRACTICE

DIRECTIONS Read each question and circle the letter of the best response.

1 How did most people in the early United States make their living?

A as laborers
B as merchants
C as craftspeople
D farming

2 What kinds of paintings were painted by members of the Hudson River School?

A portraits
B landscapes
C religious
D abstract

STANDARDS REVIEW

HSS 8.5 Students analyze U.S. foreign policy in the early Republic.

8.5.1 Understand the political and economic causes and consequences of the War of 1812 and know the major battles, leaders, and events that led to a final peace.

British officers began stopping and searching American ships for runaway British sailors. When the British forced these runaways to return to British ships, it was called "impressment." These violations of U.S. neutrality led to the Embargo Act, which banned all trade with foreign countries. The act had a devastating effect on American merchants. In addition, many Americans believed that the British were aiding Native Americans in clashes with American settlers in the West.

These events led President James Madison to ask Congress to declare war in 1812, the first war in U.S. history. In 1813 Captain Oliver Hazard Perry defeated the British in the Battle of Lake Erie. General William Henry Harrison led an invasion of Canada. In 1814 the British attacked Washington, D.C., forcing President Madison to flee the capital. In the Battle of New Orleans, Andrew Jackson led troops that defended the city and the Mississippi River.

The War of 1812 ended in 1814. Each nation returned the territory it had conquered. The war produced intense feelings of patriotism. The power of many Native American groups was broken. The interruption of trade led to growth in American manufacturing. Most importantly, winning the war convinced Americans that their experiment in democracy would survive.

STANDARDS PRACTICE

DIRECTIONS Read each question and circle the letter of the best response.

1 How did impressment violate U.S. neutrality?

A by leading to the Embargo Act
B British officers were stopping U.S. naval vessels.
C by aiding Native Americans who fought American settlers
D It didn't affect U.S. neutrality.

2 What was the most important effect of the War of 1812?

A It convinced Americans that their democracy would survive.
B It spurred American manufacturing.
C It broke the power of many Native American groups.
D It produced intense feelings of patriotism.

STANDARDS REVIEW

HSS 8.5 Students analyze U.S. foreign policy in the early Republic.

8.5.2 Know the changing boundaries of the United States and describe the relationships the country had with its neighbors (current Mexico and Canada) and Europe, including the influence of the Monroe Doctrine, and how those relationships influenced westward expansion and the Mexican-American War.

In 1803, the Louisiana Purchase nearly doubled the size of the United States, extending its territory from the Mississippi River west to the Rocky Mountains. In 1819, the United States acquired Florida and the Oregon Country from Spain.

Before and during the War of 1812, U.S. leaders made several attempts to expand into British North America. Compromises were reached with Britain in limiting naval power on the Great Lakes, in securing fishing rights, and in sharing control of the Pacific Northwest.

The United States expanded into the new Republic of Mexico. In 1845 Congress approved the annexation of the Republic of Texas. In 1848, after the War with Mexico, the Mexican Cession gave the United States most of Mexico's northern territory, including California.

The Neutrality Proclamation of 1793 stated that the United States would not take sides with any European countries that were at war. President James Monroe became concerned that European powers might try to take control of newly independent countries in Latin America. The Monroe Doctrine of 1823 warned European colonial powers not to interfere with the Americas. In exchange, the United States would not interfere in the affairs of European nations.

STANDARDS PRACTICE

DIRECTIONS Read each question and circle the letter of the best response.

1 What was one of the outcomes of the War with Mexico?

A Texas independence
B U.S. annexation of Texas
C the Mexican Cession
D the Monroe Doctrine

2 Which acquisition nearly doubled the size of the United States?

A the Louisiana Purchase
B the acquisition of Florida and the Oregon Country
C the annexation of Texas
D the Mexican Cession

STANDARDS REVIEW

HSS 8.5 Students analyze U.S. foreign policy in the early Republic.
8.5.3 Outline the major treaties with American Indian nations during the administrations of the first four presidents and the varying outcomes of those treaties.

In August 1795, Native American leaders signed the Treaty of Greenville. It gave the United States the right of entry to lands held by Native Americans in the Northwest Territory. It also guaranteed the safety of U.S. citizens there. In exchange, Native Americans received $20,000 in goods and recognition of their claim to lands they still held.

Shawnee chief Tecumseh grew angry when he saw Native Americans being pushed off their lands. He tried to unite Native American groups in a confederation. In 1810 the governor of the Indiana Territory, William Henry Harrison, urged Tecumseh to follow the Treaty of Greenville. Tecumseh replied that no single chief had the right to sell land that had belonged to all Native Americans. Harrison then destroyed Tecumseh's village in the Battle of Tippecanoe. Along with the village, Harrison also destroyed Tecumseh's dream of a great Indian confederation.

In 1813, Creek Indians lashed out against American settlers. The commander of the Tennessee militia, Andrew Jackson, attacked them in 1814 in Alabama. The Treaty of Fort Jackson, signed later that year, forced the Creek to give up 23 million acres of their land.

STANDARDS PRACTICE

DIRECTIONS Read each question and circle the letter of the best response.

1 Tecumseh hoped to prevent the takeover of Native American lands by white settlers

A by negotiating new treaties.
B by becoming governor of the Indiana Territory.
C by forming a great Native American confederation.
D by buying the land back from white settlers.

2 Which of the following was not a provision of the Treaty of Greenville?

A It gave the United States the right to enter Native American lands.
B It guaranteed the safety of U.S. citizens in the Northwest Territory.
C Native Americans received $20,000 in payment.
D It forced Native Americans to leave the Northwest Territory.

History–Social Science Grade 8 — Standard 8.6.1

STANDARDS REVIEW

HSS 8.6 Students analyze the divergent paths of the American people from 1800 to the mid-1800s and the challenges they faced, with emphasis on the Northeast.

8.6.1 Discuss the influence of industrialization and technological developments on the region, including human modification of the landscape and how physical geography shaped human actions (e.g., growth of cities, deforestation, farming, mineral extraction).

The Northeast region had many rivers and streams to provide a reliable supply of water power for mills, and it was here that industries first developed. As steam power began to replace water power, factories could be located closer to cities and transportation centers. Cities soon became the center of industrial growth. People from rural areas and foreign countries flocked to cities to work in the factories.

New farm equipment such as the reaper and the steel plow allowed Midwestern farmers to plant and harvest huge crop fields. These new machines also reduced the number of workers required to farm.

New means of transportation such as steamboats and trains allowed manufacturers and farmers to send their goods to distant markets. Cities such as Chicago became transportation hubs.

The logging industry expanded and flourished as trees were cut to supply wood for houses and furniture, for paper, to clear land for farming, and for fuel. Eventually coal began to replace wood as a fuel source. In the 1870s the demand for coal soared to meet the growing demand for steel. Coal mining, like logging, changed the landscape. Logging led to deforestation. Coal mining left deep gashes in the earth.

STANDARDS PRACTICE

DIRECTIONS Read each question and circle the letter of the best response.

1 Where did industrialization first take place in the United States?

A in the South
B in the Northeast
C in cities
D in rural areas

2 Why did large-scale deforestation take place in the United States?

A to provide fuel
B to supply wood for houses
C to clear land for farming
D all of the above

STANDARDS REVIEW

HSS 8.6 Students analyze the divergent paths of the American people from 1800 to the mid-1800s and the challenges they faced, with emphasis on the Northeast.

8.6.2 Outline the physical obstacles to and the economic and political factors involved in building a network of roads, canals, and railroads (e.g., Henry Clay's American System).

Kentucky Representative Henry Clay developed a plan that came to be known as the American System. It was a series of measures intended to make the United States economically self-sufficient. Among the measures was a protective tariff. Clay wanted tariff money to be used to improve roads and canals. He believed that these improvements would unite the country.

In the early 1800s, land travel was difficult. Most roads in the country were made of dirt. The Cumberland Road, begun in 1815, was the first road built by the federal government. Water transportation was usually quicker, easier, and cheaper. For this reason, canals were built. Canals had to be dug by hand, and they took years to complete.

Steam-powered boats and trains revolutionized transportation. American railroads often had to run up and down steep mountains, around tight curves, and over swift rivers. Tracks, however, were built quickly, and by 1860 about 30,000 miles of railroad linked almost every major city in the eastern United States.

STANDARDS PRACTICE

DIRECTIONS Read each question and circle the letter of the best response.

1 What was the American System?

A a system of roads and canals
B a system for running factories
C a series of measures to make the U.S. economically self-sufficient
D a system of trade agreements that enabled the United States to compete with Great Britain

2 What new forms of transportation appeared in the early 1800s?

A sailing ships
B steamboats and trains
C horse-drawn carts
D gasoline-powered trucks

Name ______________________ Class ______________ Date ______________

History–Social Science Grade 8 — Standard 8.6.3

STANDARDS REVIEW

HSS 8.6 Students analyze the divergent paths of the American people from 1800 to the mid-1800s and the challenges they faced, with emphasis on the Northeast.

8.6.3 List the reasons for the wave of immigration from Northern Europe to the United States and describe the growth in the number, size, and spatial arrangements of cities (e.g., Irish immigrants and the Great Irish Famine).

Between 1840 and 1860, more than four million immigrants came to the United States from Europe. More than three million of these immigrants came from Ireland and Germany. More than a million Irish people fled to the United States when a potato blight caused a famine in Ireland in the mid-1840s. Most Irish immigrants were very poor. Many settled in cities and towns in the Northeast. They worked at unskilled jobs in the cities or building canals and railroads. Women often took jobs working as servants for wealthy families. Most Germans came for economic reasons as well. The United States seemed to offer greater economic opportunity and more freedom from government control. Unlike the Irish, many German immigrants went to Midwestern states. Land was more available than in the Northeast, and they became farmers. Other German immigrants worked as tailors, bricklayers, servants, clerks, cabinetmakers, bakers, and food merchants in urban centers.

As the Transportation Revolution connected cities, people moved about in large numbers. They were drawn by the many new jobs created by the Industrial Revolution. Three-quarters of the country's manufacturing jobs were in Northeastern and mid-Atlantic regions. Populations in cities in these areas grew the most.

STANDARDS PRACTICE

DIRECTIONS Read each question and circle the letter of the best response.

1 Where did most of the Irish immigrants to the U.S. settle?

A in the Northeast
B in the South
C in Midwestern states
D in the West

2 Why did most Germans come to the United States?

A because of a famine
B for economic reasons
C to avoid military service
D to escape political oppression

STANDARDS REVIEW

HSS 8.6 Students analyze the divergent paths of the American people from 1800 to the mid-1800s and the challenges they faced, with emphasis on the Northeast.

8.6.4 Study the lives of black Americans who gained freedom in the North and founded schools and churches to advance their rights and communities.

In the 1700s and early 1800s, free African Americans were usually prohibited from attending the same schools as white students. The New York African Free School educated hundreds of children, many of whom became brilliant scholars and important African American leaders. Philadelphia had a long history of accepting and providing education for African Americans. By 1800 the city ran seven schools for African Americans. In 1820, Boston opened a separate elementary school for African American children. The city began to allow African Americans to attend white schools in 1855.

In 1835 Oberlin became the first college to accept African American students. It was followed by Harvard and Dartmouth. Then in 1842 the Institute for Colored Youth opened in Philadelphia.

Many free African Americans opened and joined churches. The African Methodist Episcopal Church spread across the Middle Atlantic states. By 1820 there were about 4,000 African American Methodists in Philadelphia. Some former slaves even became Baptist, Methodist, or Presbyterian ministers. They often became active in the anti-slavery movement. One former slave who became a leader in the anti-slavery movement was Frederick Douglass, who gained fame for his speeches denouncing slavery.

STANDARDS PRACTICE

DIRECTIONS Read each question and circle the letter of the best response.

1 In 1800 which city had seven schools for African Americans?

A Boston
B New York
C Philadelphia
D none of the above

2 What was the first college to admit African Americans?

A Dartmouth
B Harvard
C Oberlin
D Institute for Colored Youth

STANDARDS REVIEW

HSS 8.6 Students analyze the divergent paths of the American people from 1800 to the mid-1800s and the challenges they faced, with emphasis on the Northeast.

8.6.5 Trace the development of the American education system from its earliest roots, including the roles of religious and private schools and Horace Mann's campaign for free public education and its assimilating role in American culture.

In the early 1800s, the availability of education varied widely from region to region. New England had the largest number of schools. The South and West had the fewest. Few teachers were trained, and schools were small. Students of all ages and levels usually worked in one room.

Social background and wealth affected the quality of education. Rich families sent children to private schools or hired tutors. Poor children attended public schools, if there was one in their area. Girls could go to school, but parents often did not see any reason for educating them.

Horace Mann, an educational reformer, was a leader of the common-school movement. He thought that education made children responsible citizens. Mann called for all children to be taught in a common place, regardless of background.

As Massachusetts' first Secretary for Education, Mann doubled the state's school budget and raised teachers' salaries. He lengthened the school year and began the first school for teacher training. Mann set the standard for education reform throughout the country.

STANDARDS PRACTICE

DIRECTIONS Read each question and circle the letter of the best response.

1 What was the common-school movement?

- **A** the same education for all children, regardless of their background
- **B** education for boys only
- **C** education for the rich only
- **D** education for whites only

2 What did Horace Mann do to improve education?

- **A** He raised teachers' salaries.
- **B** He lengthened the school year.
- **C** He began the first school for teacher training.
- **D** all of the above

STANDARDS REVIEW

HSS 8.6 Students analyze the divergent paths of the American people from 1800 to the mid-1800s and the challenges they faced, with emphasis on the Northeast.

8.6.6 Examine the women's suffrage movement (e.g., biographies, writings, and speeches of Elizabeth Cady Stanton, Margaret Fuller, Lucretia Mott, Susan B. Anthony).

Social changes led to the rise of the woman's movement. Women took advantage of better educational opportunities. Many women took an active part in reform and abolition efforts. Many activists began to find it unacceptable that women were not allowed to vote, and often they were not even allowed to control their own property.

Women found that they had to defend their right to speak in public, especially when the audience included men. Women, however, began to speak out. In 1845 a woman named Margaret Fuller wrote a book in which she said that women had the right to choose their own paths in life. In 1848 Elizabeth Cady Stanton and her friend Lucretia Mott organized the Seneca Falls Convention. It was the first organized public meeting about women's rights in the United States. The organizers wrote a Declaration of Sentiments that detailed their beliefs about social injustice toward women. Susan B. Anthony was another important female suffragette. She argued that women and men should receive equal pay for equal work. She also believed that women should be allowed to enter traditionally male professions such as religion and law.

STANDARDS PRACTICE

DIRECTIONS Read each question and circle the letter of the best response.

1 How did early American women find their rights to be limited?

A They were not allowed to marry.
B They were not allowed to vote.
C They were not allowed to get an education.
D They were not allowed to work.

2 Why is Susan B. Anthony important?

A She invented the dollar coin.
B She was the first woman Secretary of Education.
C She argued that women and men should receive equal pay for equal work.
D She wrote the Declaration of Sentiments.

STANDARDS REVIEW

HSS 8.6 Students analyze the divergent paths of the American people from 1800 to the mid-1800s and the challenges they faced, with emphasis on the Northeast.

8.6.7 Identify common themes in American art as well as transcendentalism and individualism (e.g., writings about and by Ralph Waldo Emerson, Henry David Thoreau, Herman Melville, Louisa May Alcott, Nathaniel Hawthorne, Henry Wadsworth Longfellow).

Some New England writers and philosophers were inspired by the idea of transcendentalism. They believed that people could transcend, or rise above, material things. They believed that people should depend on their own insights rather than outside authorities.

Ralph Waldo Emerson wrote an essay called "Self-Reliance." In this essay he said that Americans relied too much on institutions. Instead, they should follow their personal beliefs and use their judgment. Henry David Thoreau also believed in self-reliance. He summarized many of his ideas in his book *Walden*, which was published in 1854.

One of the best-known pieces of American literature is *The Scarlet Letter* by Nathaniel Hawthorne. It describes Puritan life in the 1600s. Hawthorne's friend Herman Melville wrote tales of the sea, such as *Moby-Dick* and *Billy Budd*. Many people consider *Moby-Dick* to be one of the greatest American novels ever written.

Henry Wadsworth Longfellow was the best known poet of the mid-1800s. He wrote popular story-poems like *Hiawatha*. Another poet, Walt Whitman, first published *Leaves of Grass* in 1855. He praised American individualism and democracy in his simple, unrhymed poetry.

STANDARDS PRACTICE

DIRECTIONS Read each question and circle the letter of the best response.

1 What was transcendentalism?

A a belief in the spirit world

B a belief that people should rely on opinions of known authorities

C a belief that people should rise above material things

D a belief in the equality of races

2 What poet praised American individualism and democracy?

A Walt Whitman

B Henry Wadsworth Longfellow

C Ralph Waldo Emerson

D Henry David Thoreau

STANDARDS REVIEW

HSS 8.7 Students analyze the divergent paths of the American people in the South from 1800 to the mid-1800s and the challenges they faced.

8.7.1 Describe the development of the agrarian economy in the South, identify the locations of the cotton-producing states, and discuss the significance of cotton and the cotton gin.

Many southerners believed that the future of the United States was dependent on agriculture. After the American Revolution, however, prices for major southern crops such as rice and tobacco fell. Some landowners cut production or switched to crops that needed less labor. As a result, the cost of slaves fell.

Southerners had been growing small amounts of cotton since the founding of Jamestown, Virginia, in 1607. When Southerners discovered how profitable cotton could be, it became a major crop. Growing and processing cotton was labor intensive, so slavery increased. In 1793, Northerner Eli Whitney patented the cotton gin. The cotton gin was a machine that removed the seeds from cotton. As a result, cotton could be processed much faster than it was by hand. Whitney's invention sparked a cotton boom.

Cotton had many advantages as a cash crop. It cost little to market. Unlike food staples, it could be stored for a long time. Because it was lighter than other staple crops, it cost less to transport over long distances. In addition, the textile industry in the northeastern states and in Great Britain created a high demand for cotton.

A cotton belt stretched from South Carolina to Texas. Most of the country's cotton was grown in this region. Many farmers grew little else. In the South, it was declared, "Cotton is King!"

STANDARDS PRACTICE

DIRECTIONS Read each question and circle the letter of the best response.

1 Many southerners believed the future of the United States depended

A on agriculture.

B on the textile industry.

C on cotton.

D on slavery.

2 A cotton boom occurred because

A of the increase in slavery.

B of the expansion of the United States territory.

C cotton was cheap to transport over long distances.

D the invention of the cotton gin made cotton easier to process.

STANDARDS REVIEW

HSS 8.7 Students analyze the divergent paths of the American people in the South from 1800 to the mid-1800s and the challenges they faced.

8.7.2 Trace the origins and development of slavery; its effects on black Americans and on the region's political, social, religious, economic, and cultural development; and identify the strategies that were tried to both overturn and preserve it (e.g., through the writings and historical documents on Nat Turner, Denmark Vesey).

The first Africans came to Virginia on a Dutch ship in 1619. Some Africans were servants, while others had been enslaved. When the cost of slaves began to fall, many wealthy farmers with large plantations turned to slave labor. The cotton boom resulted in a major increase in the slave trade. Most slaves received inadequate food, clothing and shelter. Strict laws called slave codes controlled their actions. Life for enslaved Africans was brutal. Many found comfort in their community and in their culture. Family was important. So was religion. Many slaves became Christian, and some enslaved people began to sing spirituals to express their religious beliefs. Slaves eventually blended some aspects of traditional African religions with those of Christianity.

Violent slave revolts were rare, but white southerners lived in constant fear of them. Anti-slavery writers called Denmark Vesey a hero after he was executed for allegedly plotting a violent slave uprising. The most violent slave revolt occurred in 1831. Nat Turner, a Virginia slave, led a group of slaves in a plan to kill slaveholders and their families. They killed about 60 white people in the community. More than 100 innocent slaves were killed in an attempt to stop the rebellion. Turner was eventually caught and executed. Stemming from the Turner Rebellion, new slave codes were established that placed stricter controls on slaves.

STANDARDS PRACTICE

DIRECTIONS Read each question and circle the letter of the best response.

1 Why did the slave trade increase?

A Dutch traders
B slave codes
C the cotton boom
D shortage of laborers

2 What was one result of Nat Turner's revolt?

A New slave codes were enacted.
B Slavery was abolished.
C The slave trade increased.
D Denmark Vesey was proclaimed a hero.

STANDARDS REVIEW

HSS 8.7 Students analyze the divergent paths of the American people in the South from 1800 to the mid-1800s and the challenges they faced.
8.7.3 Examine the characteristics of white Southern society and how the physical environment influenced events and conditions prior to the Civil War.

Sectional differences had always existed between the different regions of the United States. These differences became deeper as the North experienced major changes in industry and transportation, while the South remained mainly agricultural.

The romantic view of life in the South was not a reality. During the first half of the 1800s, only about one-third of white families living in the South had slaves. However, the planters who held slaves had a powerful influence. They were the wealthiest members of society, and many were political leaders. Some lived in beautiful mansions and had large land holdings.

Most white southerners owned small farms. They took pride in their work, and their families worked long days at a variety of tasks. Very few earned enough money to buy slaves. The poorest white southerners made up less than 10 percent of the white population. Generally, they lived on land that could not grow cash crops. They hunted, fished, raised small gardens, and did odd jobs for money.

Many of the South's largest cities were shipping centers located along the Atlantic coast. There were fewer cities than in the North, but they were similar. They had public water systems and well-maintained streets. As on plantations, slaves did much of the work in cities. They worked as servants, in mills, in shipyards, and at skilled jobs.

STANDARDS PRACTICE

DIRECTIONS Read each question and circle the letter of the best response.

1 In the early 1800s, how many white families owned slaves in the South?

A most
B about half
C about one-third
D fewer than 10 percent

2 What group formed the largest part of the southern white population?

A owners of small farms
B poor people
C plantation owners
D city dwellers

STANDARDS REVIEW

HSS 8.7 Students analyze the divergent paths of the American people in the South from 1800 to the mid-1800s and the challenges they faced.
8.7.4 Compare the lives of and opportunities for free blacks in the North with those of free blacks in the South.

Free African Americans who lived in cities worked in a variety of jobs, mostly as skilled artisans or craftspeople. A few became quite successful in their businesses. In rural areas, free African Americans often worked for plantations and farmers. Churches often served as the center of their social life. Free African Americans in the North had opportunities for education, although they usually did not attend the same schools as white students. In Boston, African Americans were not allowed to attend white schools until 1855.

Free African Americans faced discrimination in both the North and the South, but it was especially harsh in the South. Only in New England could African Americans vote. Although many free African Americans were landowners, laws limited where they could live, what they could do for work, and with whom they could meet. In some places, laws dictated that a white person had to represent African Americans in their business dealings.

By 1860 more than half of all free African Americans lived in the South. Some were descendants of slaves who had been freed after the American Revolution. Others had worked to buy their freedom. In 1806, Virginia passed a law banning former slaves from living in the state without special permission. Some white southerners feared that free African Americans would try to encourage slave rebellions.

STANDARDS PRACTICE

DIRECTIONS Read each question and circle the letter of the best response.

1 In the early 1800s African Americans could vote in

A all the states.
B none of the states.
C in New England.
D in the Western states.

2 In 1860, in what part of the United States did most of the free African Americans live?

A the Northeast
B the South
C the Midwest
D the West

Name ______________________ Class ______________ Date ______________

STANDARDS REVIEW

HSS 8.8 Students analyze the divergent paths of the American people in the West from 1800 to the mid-1800s and the challenges they faced.
8.8.1 Discuss the election of Andrew Jackson as president in 1828, the importance of Jacksonian democracy, and his actions as president (e.g., the spoils system, veto of the National Bank, policy of Indian removal, opposition to the Supreme Court).

Beginning in the 1790s, state legislatures made efforts to give more people the right to vote. New states allowed all white men to vote. Political parties began to give people more say in choosing candidates. This expansion of voting rights came to be called Jacksonian Democracy. It was named for Andrew Jackson, who benefited from these efforts. Jackson was a popular war hero who was running for president. His supporters were mostly farmers, frontier settlers, and slaveholders. They believed he would defend their rights. Once elected president, Jackson rewarded some of his supporters with government jobs. This practice became known as the spoils system.

As president, Jackson questioned the legality of the Second Bank of the United States. Although the Supreme Court had ruled that the Bank was constitutional, Jackson vetoed legislation to renew its charter.

Under pressure from Jackson, Congress passed the Indian Removal Act. It called for the removal of Native Americans who lived east of the Mississippi River to lands in the West. The Supreme Court ruled that the Cherokee nation could not be removed from its lands by the state of Georgia. When Georgia ignored the Court's ruling, U.S. troops began to remove the Cherokee in the spring of 1838.

STANDARDS PRACTICE

DIRECTIONS Read each question and circle the letter of the best response.

1 The term Jacksonian Democracy refers to

A the erosion of voting rights.
B the expansion of voting rights.
C a political party.
D the spoils system.

2 Under the Indian Removal Act, Native Americans were moved to

A lands east of the Mississippi
B Georgia
C lands west of the Mississippi
D the Northeast

STANDARDS REVIEW

HSS 8.8 Students analyze the divergent paths of the American people in the West from 1800 to the mid-1800s and the challenges they faced.

8.8.2 Describe the purpose, challenges, and economic incentives associated with westward expansion, including the concept of Manifest Destiny (e.g., the Lewis and Clark expedition, accounts of the removal of Indians, the Cherokees' "Trail of Tears," settlement of the Great Plains) and the territorial acquisitions that spanned numerous decades.

President Thomas Jefferson asked Congress to fund an expedition to explore lands acquired in the Louisiana Purchase. Meriwether Lewis and William Clark led this famous expedition. They took about 50 skilled frontiersmen in their Corps of Discovery. The group used the Missouri River as their highway through the Great Plains. They crossed the Rocky Mountains and followed the Columbia River to the Pacific.

In 1830 Congress passed the Indian Removal Act. It called for the removal of Native Americans who lived east of the Mississippi River to lands in the West. The Choctaw were the first sent to the new Indian Territory. Other groups were then forced to move. The Cherokee who lived in Georgia believed they could avoid removal by adopting white culture. However, when gold was found on their land, Georgia's leaders forced them off. Nearly one fourth of the Cherokee died on an 800-mile forced march that is known as the Trail of Tears.

By the 1840s, the United States had a booming economy, a growing population, and a belief that the country needed more room. Some Americans believed that it was their manifest destiny to conquer lands all the way to the Pacific Ocean. Many settlers moved west over the Oregon Trail, which started at the Missouri River, crossed the Rocky Mountains, and branched to end either in Oregon or in California.

STANDARDS PRACTICE

DIRECTIONS Read each question and circle the letter of the best response.

1 Where did Lewis and Clark explore?

A the Great Plains
B the Rocky Mountains
C both A and B
D neither A nor B

2 What was the Trail of Tears?

A the route followed by Lewis and Clark
B the route followed by the Cherokee in their forced march
C the Oregon Trail
D the Santa Fe Trail

STANDARDS REVIEW

HSS 8.8 Students analyze the divergent paths of the American people in the West from 1800 to the mid-1800s and the challenges they faced.
8.8.3 Describe the role of pioneer women and the new status that western women achieved (e.g., Laura Ingalls Wilder, Annie Bidwell; slave women gaining freedom in the West; Wyoming granting suffrage to women in 1869).

Women in particular found the journey along the Oregon Trail miserable. Fashion required them to be clothed from head to toe, but life on the trail took its toll. Only about five percent of gold-rush immigrants were women or children. Some married women made the journey to California with their husbands. These hardworking wives generally made good money for their families by cooking meals, washing clothes, and opening boardinghouses for single male settlers.

Biddy Mason and her family arrived in California as slaves during the gold-rush years. Biddy quickly discovered that most Californians opposed slavery. She and her family gained their freedom and moved to the small village of Los Angeles, where she managed to purchase some land. Over time, her property increased in value from $250 to $200,000. She became one of the wealthiest landowners in California, a community leader, and a well-known supporter of charities.

Author Laura Ingalls Wilder was one of four children in a pioneer family. Her books about settlers' lives on the prairie are still popular today. Another well-known pioneer woman was Annie Bidwell. Bidwell supported a number of moral and social causes, including the movement for women's suffrage.

STANDARDS PRACTICE

DIRECTIONS Read each question and circle the letter of the best response.

1 Who was Biddy Mason?

A a former slave
B a wealthy California property owner
C a community leader
D all of the above

2 Why is Annie Bidwell remembered?

A She was a former slave who became successful.
B She wrote about settlers' lives on the prairie.
C She worked for women's suffrage.
D She opened a boardinghouse.

Name ______________________ Class ______________ Date ______________

History–Social Science Grade 8 — Standard 8.8.4

STANDARDS REVIEW

HSS 8.8 Students analyze the divergent paths of the American people in the West from 1800 to the mid-1800s and the challenges they faced.
8.8.4 Examine the importance of the great rivers and the struggle over water rights.

In the early days of the United States, rivers provided water power to run mills in the Northeast. In addition, rivers such as the Hudson, the Ohio, and the Mississippi served as the nation's highways. Lewis and Clark followed the Missouri and the Columbia rivers to explore the territories stemming from the Louisiana Purchase.

In the East, water-use laws commonly required owners whose land bordered streams or rivers to maintain a free flow of water downstream. These restrictions generally prevented landowners from constructing dams. Building dams would infringe upon the water rights of neighbors.

In the generally dry climate of the West, large-scale agriculture was not possible without irrigation. Dams and canals were required to direct the scarce water to the fields. This need was very different from the accepted eastern tradition of equal access to water.

Brigham Young, who lived in Utah and was president of the Mormon Church, established a strict code regulating water rights for the Mormon community. In any dispute over water use, the good of the community would outweigh the interests of individuals. This approach, with its emphasis on the needs of the community, stood as an example for modern water laws throughout the West.

STANDARDS PRACTICE

DIRECTIONS Read each question and circle the letter of the best response.

1 Which kind of water use would generally be restricted in the East?

- **A** dam construction
- **B** transportation
- **C** irrigation
- **D** water power for mills

2 What group's water rights served as an example throughout the West?

- **A** the Native Americans
- **B** the Mormons
- **C** the Mexicans
- **D** the ranchers

STANDARDS REVIEW

HSS 8.8 Students analyze the divergent paths of the American people in the West from 1800 to the mid-1800s and the challenges they faced.

8.8.5 Discuss Mexican settlements and their locations, cultural traditions, attitudes toward slavery, land-grant system, and economies.

After Mexico became independent in 1821, the government hired agents called *empresarios* to bring settlers to Texas. Americans began building colonies in Texas, but their ties remained with the United States. One young agent, Stephen F. Austin, received permission to start a colony on the lower Colorado River in 1822. He chose settlers carefully. The first 300 families became known as the Old Three Hundred. Each received 640 acres, with an extra 320 acres for each child in the family.

Austin's success in establishing a colony attracted other agents, and American settlers poured into the region. In exchange for free land, settlers had to become Mexican citizens, obey Mexican laws, and practice the official religion of Mexico, Roman Catholicism. But settlers often ignored Mexican laws. For example, although the Mexican constitution banned slavery, many settlers brought slaves.

Concerned that it was losing control to the growing American population, Mexico responded. In 1830 it banned further settlement by Americans and outlawed the importation of slaves. These actions angered many United States Texas settlers.

STANDARDS PRACTICE

DIRECTIONS Read each question and circle the letter of the best response.

1 What was an *empresario?*

A a Mexican rebel

B one of the Old Three Hundred

C an agent hired to bring settlers to Texas

D a settler who illegally brought slaves into Texas

2 What did Mexico do that angered many Texans?

A It established an official religion.

B It banned the importation of slaves.

C It forced American settlers to leave Texas.

D It forced American settlers in Texas to stop speaking English.

History–Social Science Grade 8 Standard 8.8.6

STANDARDS REVIEW

HSS 8.8 Students analyze the divergent paths of the American people in the West from 1800 to the mid-1800s and the challenges they faced.

8.8.6 Describe the Texas War for Independence and the Mexican-American War, including territorial settlements, the aftermath of the wars, and the effects the wars had on the lives of Americans, including Mexican Americans today.

After Texas declared independence in 1836, the Mexican dictator, General Antonio López de Santa Anna, attacked a Texan stronghold at the Alamo, killing all the Texans. In the subsequent Battle of San Jacinto, Santa Anna was captured and was forced to grant Texas independence. Most Texans hoped that the United States would annex Texas and make it a state. The United States Congress also wanted to annex Texas. However, President Andrew Jackson refused. He was concerned that admitting Texas as a slave state would upset the balance of free and slave states. Nor did he want a war with Mexico.

In 1845 Texas was finally annexed by the United States, triggering the Mexican War. At the beginning of the war, the U.S. Army was better equipped, but it was greatly outnumbered. The government put out a call for 50,000 volunteers, and some 200,000 responded. However, not all Americans supported the war. Many Whigs thought the war was unjustified and avoidable. Northern abolitionists opposed it because they feared the spread of slavery into southwestern lands.

The war ended after U.S. troops took Mexico City. Under the 1848 Treaty of Guadalupe Hidalgo, Mexico turned over more than 500,000 square miles of its northern territory to the United States, including California. In exchange, the United States paid Mexico $15 million.

STANDARDS PRACTICE

DIRECTIONS Read each question and circle the letter of the best response.

1 Who wanted the United States to annex Texas?

A Santa Anna
B Andrew Jackson
C United States Congress
D abolitionists

2 What was Jackson afraid would happen if the U.S. annexed Texas?

A Slavery would spread to the North.
B The balance between free and slave states would be upset.
C He would not get re-elected.
D It would bankrupt the country.

History–Social Science Grade 8 — Standard 8.9.1

STANDARDS REVIEW

HSS 8.9 Students analyze the early and steady attempts to abolish slavery and to realize the ideals of the Declaration of Independence.

8.9.1 Describe the leaders of the movement (e.g., John Quincy Adams and his proposed constitutional amendment, John Brown and the armed resistance, Harriet Tubman and the Underground Railroad, Benjamin Franklin, Theodore Weld, William Lloyd Garrison, Frederick Douglass).

The Quakers were among the first groups to oppose slavery on religious grounds, and they began working for abolition in colonial times. In the 1830s, however, Americans who opposed slavery began to take organized action to abolish slavery in the United States. These abolitionists came from many backgrounds. They reminded people of the words in the Declaration of Independence and the fact that the American Revolution had been fought in the name of equality.

Antislavery reformers did not always agree on how much equality African Americans should have. Some thought African Americans should have the same rights as white citizens, while others were against full political and social equality.

Some wanted to send freed African Americans to Africa to start new colonies in order to avoid conflicts between the races in the United States. In 1817, a minister named Robert Finley started the American Colonization Society. Five years later, this society founded the colony of Liberia on the western coast of Africa. About 12,000 African Americans eventually settled there.

STANDARDS PRACTICE

DIRECTIONS Read each question and circle the letter of the best response.

1 What religious group was among the first to oppose slavery?

A the Pilgrims
B the Puritans
C the Quakers
D the American Colonization Society

2 Where did the American Colonization Society hope to resettle freed African Americans?

A in Africa
B in Canada
C in the North
D in the Northwest Territory

STANDARDS REVIEW

Abolitionists found many ways to further their cause. William Lloyd Garrison began an abolitionist newspaper, the *Liberator*, which first appeared in 1831. In 1833 Garrison helped found the American Anti-Slavery Society. Its members wanted immediate emancipation of enslaved African Americans and racial equality.

Many former slaves were active in the antislavery cause. Frederick Douglass escaped from slavery when he was 20. He became one of the most important African American leaders of the 1800s. He had secretly learned to read and write as a boy. His public-speaking skills impressed members of the Anti-Slavery Society, and in 1841 they asked him to give regular lectures.

By the 1830s, a loosely organized group had begun helping slaves escape from the South. Free African Americans, former slaves, and a few white abolitionists worked together to create the Underground Railroad. The organization was a network of people who arranged transportation and hiding places for fugitive slaves. The people who led the fugitives were known as conductors. The most famous and daring conductor was Harriet Tubman. She escaped from slavery in 1849, and went on to lead more than 300 other slaves to freedom.

In 1858 John Brown tried to start a slave uprising. He wanted to attack the federal arsenal in Virginia and seize weapons there. He planned to arm local slaves and kill or imprison white southerners who stood in his way. However, African Americans did not come to his aid. Instead, local white southerners attacked Brown at Harper's Ferry, Virginia. Brown was arrested and quickly tried. After his execution, many northern abolitionists mourned Brown's death.

STANDARDS PRACTICE

DIRECTIONS Read each question and circle the letter of the best response.

3 Who founded the abolitionist newspaper, the *Liberator?*

A Frederick Douglass
B John Brown
C Harriett Tubman
D William Lloyd Garrison

4 The Underground Railroad was

A an organization that tried to start slave uprisings.
B an organization that helped educate former slaves.
C a network of people who helped slaves escape.
D none of the above

STANDARDS REVIEW

HSS 8.9 Students analyze the early and steady attempts to abolish slavery and to realize the ideals of the Declaration of Independence.

8.9.2 Discuss the abolition of slavery in early state constitutions.

> We hold these truths to be self-evident, that all men are created equal, that they are endowed by their Creator with certain unalienable Rights, that among these are Life, Liberty, and the pursuit of Happiness. That to secure these Rights, Governments are instituted among Men, deriving their just powers from the consent of the governed, That whenever any Form of Government becomes destructive of these ends, it is the Right of the People to alter or to abolish it, and to institute new Government, laying its foundations on such principles and organizing its powers in such form, as to them shall seem most likely to effect their Safety and Happiness.
>
> from *The Declaration of Independence*

The Declaration of Independence did not recognize the rights of enslaved African Americans. In July 1776 slavery was legal in all of the colonies. The Revolution raised questions for some colonists about whether slavery should exist in a land that valued liberty. Some Patriot writers had said that living under British rule was similar to living a life of slavery. The difference between the ideals of liberty and the practice of slavery was a subject of great disagreement among Americans.

STANDARDS PRACTICE

DIRECTIONS Read each question and circle the letter of the best response.

1 According to the Declaration of Independence, what kind of a right is liberty?

A a civil right
B a human right
C a universal right
D an unalienable right

2 To what did some Patriot writers compare living under British rule?

A death
B slavery
C freedom
D liberty

STANDARDS REVIEW

During the American Revolution, nearly every colony wrote a new state constitution. These constitutions supported republicanism. In a republic, citizens elect representatives who are responsible to the people who elected them. Most state constitutions had rules to protect the rights of citizens. Some banned slavery. Many states' constitutions expanded suffrage, or voting rights. Seven state constitutions gave suffrage to free African American men. By the 1860s, however, these rights had been either taken away or greatly limited.

By the 1780s, the New England colonies were taking steps to end slavery. Even so, the conflict over slavery continued long after the Revolutionary War ended.

The Northwest Ordinance of 1787 stated that "there shall be neither slavery nor involuntary servitude in the . . . territory." This meant that slavery was banned in the Northwest Territory. This law was based on a proposal by Thomas Jefferson. However, unlike the Northwestern Territories, when Texas gained independence from Mexico in 1836, it modeled both its declaration and constitution after those of the United States. The only difference being that the Texas constitution specifically made slavery legal. Thus, when Texas was admitted to the Union in 1845, it joined as a slave state.

STANDARDS PRACTICE

DIRECTIONS Read each question and circle the letter of the best response.

3 What law banned slavery in the Northwest Territory?

A the Declaration of Independence
B the Articles of Confederation
C the Constitution
D the Northwest Ordinance of 1787

4 What major difference was there between the Texas constitution and the U.S. Constitution on which it was based?

A The Texas constitution was written in Spanish and English.
B The Texas constitution specifically banned slavery.
C The Texas constitution explicitly legalized slavery.
D none of the above

STANDARDS REVIEW

HSS 8.9 Students analyze the early and steady attempts to abolish slavery and to realize the ideals of the Declaration of Independence.

8.9.3 Describe the significance of the Northwest Ordinance in education and in the banning of slavery in new states north of the Ohio River.

After the United States gained its independence, the Confederation Congress had to decide what to do with the western lands that fell under its control. To form a political system for the region, Congress passed the Northwest Ordinance of 1787. The ordinance established the Northwest Territory, which included the area that is now Illinois, Indiana, Michigan, Ohio, and Wisconsin. The Northwest Ordinance said that the territory would be settled and eventually become part of the United States.

The ordinance had a bill of rights to protect settlers' civil liberties. It made education a basic right because it required that public education be provided for the citizens of the region. The ordinance also stated that "there shall be neither slavery nor involuntary servitude in the . . . territory." This meant that slavery was banned in the Northwest Territory, and it set the standard for future territories. The slavery law of the ordinance was based on a proposal made by Thomas Jefferson. However, the issue of slavery would continue to be controversial.

STANDARDS PRACTICE

DIRECTIONS Read each question and circle the letter of the best response.

1 Which of the following states came from the Northwest Territory?

A Oregon
B Illinois
C Missouri
D Washington

2 Who proposed the law banning slavery in the Northwest Territory?

A George Washington
B Benjamin Franklin
C Thomas Jefferson
D Abraham Lincoln

STANDARDS REVIEW

The Fugitive Slave Act made it a crime to help runaway slaves. It also allowed officials to arrest enslaved African Americans who were found in free areas. Slaveholders had to prove ownership of the arrested individuals, but African Americans who were accused of being fugitives were not permitted to testify. Thousands of African Americans living in the North fled to Canada. They were afraid that they would be returned to slaveholders. People who hid or helped runaway slaves faced six months in jail and a $1,000 fine. The Fugitive Slave Act upset abolitionists and most northerners.

> **Art. 6.** There shall be neither slavery nor involuntary servitude in the said territory, otherwise than in the punishment of crimes whereof the party shall have been duly convicted: Provided, always, That any person escaping into the same, from whom labor or service is lawfully claimed in any one of the original States, such fugitive may be lawfully reclaimed and conveyed to the person claiming his or her labor or service as aforesaid.
>
> from *The Northwest Ordinance of 1787*

STANDARDS PRACTICE

DIRECTIONS Read each question and circle the letter of the best response.

3 After the Fugitive Slave Act was passed, how did many northern African Americans react?

- **A** They returned to their plantations.
- **B** They went to the Northwest Territory.
- **C** They fled to Canada.
- **D** They went into hiding.

4 What did the Northwest Ordinance of 1787 have in common with the Fugitive Slave Act?

- **A** Both specified severe penalties for anyone who helped runaway slaves.
- **B** Both allowed fugitive slaves to be captured and returned to their owners.
- **C** both A and B
- **D** neither A nor B

STANDARDS REVIEW

HSS 8.9 Students analyze the early and steady attempts to abolish slavery and to realize the ideals of the Declaration of Independence.
8.9.4 Discuss the importance of the slavery issue as raised by the annexation of Texas and California's admission to the union as a free state under the Compromise of 1850.

Texas gained independence from Mexico in 1836. It modeled both its declaration and constitution after those of the United States. However, the Texas constitution specifically made slavery legal. Most Texan citizens hoped that the United States would annex Texas, making it a state. Texas politicians hoped that joining the United States would help solve the republic's financial and military problems. The United States Congress also wanted to annex Texas. But President Andrew Jackson refused. He was concerned that if Texas joined the Union, the fragile balance between free and slave states in the Union would be disrupted.

Several presidents got caught up in the tricky issue of westward expansion. John Tyler, a pro-slavery Whig from Virginia, wanted to annex Texas and thereby increase the power of the southern slave states. The next president, former Tennessee governor James K. Polk, also favored annexing Texas. By March 1845, Congress had approved the annexation. When Texas was admitted to the Union in 1845, it joined as a slave state.

STANDARDS PRACTICE

DIRECTIONS Read each question and circle the letter of the best response.

1 President Andrew Jackson refused to annex Texas because he

A was opposed to slavery.
B did not want to start a civil war.
C didn't want to upset the balance between free and slave states.
D was afraid Texas would have too much power because of its size.

2 Why did Texas politicians hope to join the United States?

A to keep Mexico from taking it back
B so that English could become the official language
C so that slavery could be made legal
D so that it could solve its financial and military problems

STANDARDS REVIEW

Mexico reacted quickly to the annexation of Texas. Mexico cut off diplomatic ties with the United States and ordered American settlers to leave California. When U.S. troops entered the disputed region between the Nueces River and the Rio Grande, war broke out between the two nations. When the war ended, Mexico turned over much of its northern territory to the United States in 1848. This land is known as the Mexican Cession. It included all of California and all or part of several other states. In exchange for the territory, the United States agreed to pay Mexico $15 million.

President Polk wanted to divide the Mexican Cession into two parts—one free and one where slavery would be legal. Some northerners wanted to prohibit slavery in all parts of the Mexican Cession. Most Californians were against slavery. Slavery had been illegal when the state was part of Mexico. Also, many forty-niners had come from free states. But, if California were made free, the balance between free and slave states would change—a change unacceptable to Southerners.

Senator Henry Clay of Kentucky introduced the Compromise of 1850. It allowed California to enter the Union as a free state. The rest of the Mexican Cession was divided into two territories. The question of slavery in those territories would be decided by popular sovereignty; that is, voters would decide whether to ban or allow slavery. The Compromise also established a new fugitive slave law.

STANDARDS PRACTICE

DIRECTIONS Read each question and circle the letter of the best response.

3 Why did the United States pay Mexico $15 million after the Mexican War?

- **A** to allow Americans to use the Rio Grande
- **B** to pay for war damages
- **C** to pay for Texas
- **D** to pay for the Mexican Cession

4 What did the Compromise of 1850 do?

- **A** It allowed California to enter the Union as a slave state.
- **B** It divided the remaining territory of the Mexican Cession into two territories.
- **C** It did away with the new fugitive slave law.
- **D** all of the above

STANDARDS REVIEW

HSS 8.9 Students analyze the early and steady attempts to abolish slavery and to realize the ideals of the Declaration of Independence.

8.9.5 Analyze the significance of the States' Rights Doctrine, the Missouri Compromise (1820), the Wilmot Proviso (1846), the Compromise of 1850, Henry Clay's role in the Missouri Compromise and the Compromise of 1850, the Kansas-Nebraska Act (1854), the *Dred Scott* v. *Sandford* decision (1857), and the Lincoln-Douglas debates (1858).

Supporters of the states' rights doctrine believed that state power should be greater than federal power. John C. Calhoun argued that states had the right to reject any federal law they disagreed with. A major conflict arose in 1819 when Congress considered Missouri's application to enter the Union as a slave state. At the time, the Union was balanced: 11 free states and 11 slave states. In 1820 Henry Clay convinced Congress to agree to the Missouri Compromise. It allowed Missouri to join the Union as a slave state and Maine to join as a free state, keeping the balance. In addition, slavery would be banned in any new territories or states formed north of 36°30' latitude (Missouri's southern border).

In the 1840s, President James K. Polk wanted to extend the 36°30' line west. The Mexican Cession would be divided into two parts, one free and one where slavery would be legal. Some northerners wanted to ban slavery in all of the Mexican Cession. Representative David Wilmot offered the Wilmot Proviso, which said that "neither slavery nor involuntary servitude shall ever exist in any part of [the] territory." It passed in the northern-controlled House of Representatives, but not in the Senate, where the South had more power.

STANDARDS PRACTICE

DIRECTIONS Read each question and circle the letter of the best response.

1 Who supported states rights?

- **A** John C. Calhoun
- **B** Henry Clay
- **C** James K. Polk
- **D** David Wilmot

2 The Missouri Compromise was proposed by

- **A** John C. Calhoun.
- **B** Henry Clay.
- **C** James K. Polk.
- **D** David Wilmot.

STANDARDS REVIEW

As well as the Missouri Compromise, Henry Clay introduced the Compromise of 1850. It allowed California to enter the Union as a free state and divided the rest of the Mexican Cession into two territories. The question of slavery in the two territories would be decided by vote. The Compromise of 1850 also established a new fugitive slave law.

Senator Stephen Douglas of Illinois introduced the Kansas-Nebraska Act. It divided what remained of the Louisiana Purchase into two territories, Kansas and Nebraska. The voters would decide the issue of slavery in the two states. Antislavery northerners were outraged, but the measure had strong southern support. Both anti-slavery and pro-slavery groups rushed people to Kansas to vote on the slavery issue.

In 1846 an enslaved African American named Dred Scott sued for his freedom. He argued that he had become free when he went with his master and lived in free territory. The case reached the Supreme Court in 1856. Chief Justice Roger B. Taney wrote the majority opinion, which ruled on three key issues. First, Taney said that African Americans had no rights because they were not citizens. Second, Taney said that Scott's residence on free soil did not make him free. Third, he declared the Missouri Compromise was unconstitutional.

In 1858, Illinois Republicans nominated Abraham Lincoln as their candidate to the U.S. Senate. His opponent was Democrat Stephen Douglas. Lincoln challenged Douglas to a series of debates. Lincoln stressed that the central issue of the campaign was the spread of slavery in the West. He argued that the Democrats were trying to spread slavery across the nation. Douglas accused Republicans of trying to make every state free. He restated his belief in popular sovereignty.

STANDARDS PRACTICE

DIRECTIONS Read each question and circle the letter of the best response.

3 Who introduced the Kansas-Nebraska Act?

A Henry Clay
B Stephen Douglas
C Roger B. Taney
D Abraham Lincoln

4 What happened as a result of the Kansas-Nebraska Act?

A Antislavery northerners were outraged.
B Antislavery groups rushed people to Kansas.
C Pro-slavery groups rushed people to Kansas.
D all of the above

Name ______________________ Class ______________ Date ______________

History–Social Science Grade 8 — Standard 8.9.6

STANDARDS REVIEW

HSS 8.9 Students analyze the early and steady attempts to abolish slavery and to realize the ideals of the Declaration of Independence.
8.9.6 Describe the lives of free blacks and the laws that limited their freedom and economic opportunities.

There were African American communities in the North starting in the early 1800s. Northern communities usually centered on one or more of the growing number of African American churches. Though they were fewer in number, some free African Americans also lived in the South.

Free African Americans enjoyed some of the benefits of early education reform. However, they often went to separate schools from white students. The New York African Free School opened in 1787. It educated hundreds of children, many of whom became brilliant scholars and important African American leaders.

Philadelphia had a long history of acceptance of African Americans. This was largely because Philadelphia was a center of Quaker influence, and the Quakers believed in equality for all people. By 1800 the city ran seven schools for African American students. In 1820, Boston opened a separate school for African American children. The city began allowing African Americans to attend white schools in 1855. In 1835 Oberlin became the first college to accept African Americans. Harvard and Dartmouth quickly followed Oberlin's example.

STANDARDS PRACTICE

DIRECTIONS Read each question and circle the letter of the best response.

1 What served as the center of northern African American communities?

A churches
B schools
C colleges
D clubs

2 Why were African-Americans accepted in Philadelphia?

A The city was founded by free African Americans.
B The city had an ordinance banning racial discrimination.
C The city was a center of Quaker influence, and Quakers believe in equality for all people.
D all of the above

STANDARDS REVIEW

Free African Americans living in southern cities worked in a variety of jobs, most as skilled artisans or craftspeople. In rural areas, they often worked for plantations and farmers as paid day laborers. Free African Americans faced discrimination in both the North and the South, but in the South it was often especially harsh. Only in New England could free African Americans vote. Although some free blacks were landowners, laws limited where they could live, what they could do for work, and with whom they could meet. In some places, laws dictated that a white person must represent African Americans in business dealings. In 1806, Virginia passed a law banning former slaves from living in the state without special permission.

By 1860 more than half of all free African Americans lived in the South. Some were descendants of slaves who had been freed after the American Revolution. Others had worked to buy their freedom. Few southern African Americans had the chance to get an education. Laws were enacted in the South to bar most slaves from getting any education. They even banned education at the primary school level. While some southern African Americans learned to read on their own, it was usually done in secret.

Many white southerners felt that free African Americans could not take care of themselves. But African Americans proved that they could survive and thrive as free people. As a result, many white southerners viewed the free African American population as a threat to slavery.

STANDARDS PRACTICE

DIRECTIONS Read each question and circle the letter of the best response.

3 What kinds of discrimination did African Americans face?

A Laws limited where they could live.

B Laws limited what they could do for work.

C Laws limited with whom they could meet.

D all of the above

4 How did many white southerners view free African Americans?

A as equals

B as neighbors

C as a threat to slavery

D none of the above

STANDARDS REVIEW

HSS 8.10 Students analyze the multiple causes, key events, and complex consequences of the Civil War.

8.10.1 Compare the conflicting interpretations of state and federal authority as emphasized in the speeches and writings of statesmen such as Daniel Webster and John C. Calhoun.

In 1828, Congress passed a tariff on imported woolen goods. The new tariff added to the problems caused by sectional differences. Northerners wanted the new tariff because it would protect their industries from foreign competition, especially from Great Britain. Southerners opposed the tariff because it would hurt their more agrarian-based economy. These Southerners were outraged and called the tariff of 1828 the Tariff of Abominations.

Vice President John C. Calhoun joined his fellow southerners in protest. Economic depression and tariffs had hurt the economy of his home state, South Carolina, which in 1828 was just recovering from a depression. Calhoun wrote a resolution called the South Carolina Exposition and Protest. Calhoun argued that this new tariff violated the states' rights doctrine. Supporters of the states' rights doctrine believed that state power should be greater than federal power. Calhoun argued that states had the right to nullify, or reject, any federal law they disagreed with. The resulting dispute became known as the nullification crisis.

STANDARDS PRACTICE

DIRECTIONS Read each question and circle the letter of the best response.

1 What was the Tariff of Abominations?

A a tariff on goods imported from New England

B a tariff on imported woolen goods

C a tariff on exported goods

D a tariff on tobacco exports

2 What was the doctrine of states' rights?

A It stated that state and federal power were equal.

B It stated that only the states, and not the federal government, had power.

C It stated that state power should be greater than federal power.

D It stated that federal power should be greater than state power.

STANDARDS REVIEW

South Carolina tested the states' rights doctrine after Congress passed a new tariff in 1832. The state legislature passed a resolution declaring the 1828 and 1832 tariffs null and void. Some people thought that the federal government would use force to collect duties from the tariff. State officials said South Carolina would withdraw from the United States if this happened.

Many other political leaders, particularly the northern legislators, opposed the idea that states could nullify federal laws. Senator Daniel Webster of Massachusetts spoke out. He argued that the country had to stay united. He believed that national unity was much more important than states' rights.

> "If there be no protective power in the reserved rights of the states, they must in the end be forced to rebel."
>
> John C. Calhoun, Vice President to Andrew Jackson

> "Liberty and Union, now and forever, one and inseparable!"
>
> Daniel Webster, Senator from Massachusetts

STANDARDS PRACTICE

DIRECTIONS Read each question and circle the letter of the best response.

3 In the quotation by John C. Calhoun, he seems to say that

- **A** states must comply with all federal law.
- **B** if states rebel, the federal government should send in troops.
- **C** if states' rights are violated, states have the right to rebel.
- **D** the federal government cannot legislate for the states.

4 What was Daniel Webster's stand on states' rights?

- **A** States do not have any rights.
- **B** National unity is more important than states' rights.
- **C** States' rights are more important than federal rights.
- **D** Only federal rights are important.

STANDARDS REVIEW

HSS 8.10 Students analyze the multiple causes, key events, and complex consequences of the Civil War.

8.10.2 Trace the boundaries constituting the North and the South, the geographical differences between the two regions, and the differences between agrarians and industrialists.

Three regions emerged in the United States. The North included New England and the Middle Atlantic states. It also came to include states formed from the former Northwest Territory. The South included the states south of Pennsylvania. It also came to include the states south of the Ohio River. The West originally included all the territory between the original British colonies and the Mississippi River. However, the Louisiana Purchase, the Texas annexation, the Oregon Territory, the Mexican Cession, and the Gadsden Purchase soon added more territory to the western region.

As new states joined the Union, their position on slavery determined whether they were considered part of the North or part of the South. The states of Iowa, Nebraska, California, and Oregon were free states, and as such became part of the North. Arkansas, Louisiana, Texas, and Missouri joined the South as slave states.

The North's economy was based on trade and manufacturing of items such as textiles, clothing, and machinery. In New England in particular, merchants had the money to invest in new mills. More important, this region had many rivers and streams that provided a reliable supply of power to the mills. Northerners opposed the federal government's sale of public land at cheap prices. The lure of cheap land encouraged potential laborers to leave northern factory towns for the West.

STANDARDS PRACTICE

DIRECTIONS Read each question and circle the letter of the best response.

1 The North's economy was based on

A farming.

B trade and manufacturing.

C selling land.

D none of the above

2 Why did northerners oppose sale of public land at cheap prices?

A It drove property taxes down.

B It hurt farmers.

C It caused deforestation.

D It encouraged factory workers to move away from cities.

STANDARDS REVIEW

The South's economy was based on agriculture. Most farmers and planters put their profits into further developing the plantation system, not into industry. Southern farmers raised all types of crops, the most important being the cash crops cotton and tobacco. Southerners sold a large portion of their crops to foreign nations.

Because the South's industrial growth lagged behind the North's, southerners imported their manufactured goods. Tariffs raised the price of imported manufactured goods. Therefore, they affected southern farmers greatly. In addition, high tariffs angered some of the South's European trading partners. These trading partners could raise their own tariffs in retaliation. To avoid a tariff war, southerners called for low United States tariffs.

Southerners also relied on slaves, not hired labor, to work on the plantations. Maintaining the slavery system would become an increasingly controversial issue between the North and South.

In the West, the frontier economy was just emerging. Settlers supported policies such as the sale of public land that would help their farming economy. These policies would also encourage further settlement. Western farmers grew a wide variety of crops. Their biggest needs were cheap land and improvements in transportation.

STANDARDS PRACTICE

DIRECTIONS Read each question and circle the letter of the best response.

3 What was the South's economy based on?

A industry
B trade
C farming
D shipping

4 Why did southerners oppose high tariffs?

A They imported their manufactured goods.
B High tariffs angered the South's foreign trading partners.
C The South was afraid its trading partners would raise their own tariffs in retaliation.
D all of the above

STANDARDS REVIEW

HSS 8.10 Students analyze the multiple causes, key events, and complex consequences of the Civil War.

8.10.3 Identify the constitutional issues posed by the doctrine of nullification and secession and the earliest origins of that doctrine.

In 1827 northern manufacturers began to demand a tariff on imported woolen goods. Northerners believed that a tariff would help protect their industries from foreign competition, especially from Great Britain. Southerners opposed the tariff, claiming it would hurt their economy.

In 1828 Congress passed a tariff that had very high rates. Southerners were outraged and called it the Tariff of Abominations. Passage of the tariff added to existing sectional tensions.

Vice President John C. Calhoun wrote a resolution called the South Carolina Exposition and Protest. Calhoun argued that the new tariff violated the states' rights doctrine. Supporters of this doctrine believed that state power should be greater than federal power. Calhoun argued that the federal government should not favor one state or region over another. He said that states had the right to nullify any federal law they disagreed with. The dispute became known as the nullification crisis.

South Carolina tested the states' rights doctrine after Congress passed another new tariff in 1832. The state legislature passed a resolution declaring the 1828 and 1832 tariffs "null, void… [and not] binding upon this state, its officers or citizens." State officials threatened that South Carolina would secede from, or leave, the United States if the federal government tried to collect duties from the tariff.

STANDARDS PRACTICE

DIRECTIONS Read each question and circle the letter of the best response.

1 What was nullification?

A declaring a law invalid
B seceding from the United States
C refusing to obey a law
D giving states more power than the federal government

2 What did South Carolina do in response to the 1828 tariff?

A It seceded from the Union.
B It declared war on Congress.
C It passed the South Carolina Exposition and Protest.
D all of the above

STANDARDS REVIEW

During the election of 1860, Northern and Southern Democrats could not agree on a presidential candidate. One result was that a new political party, the Constitutional Union Party, emerged. Another result was that the Republican candidate, Abraham Lincoln, won 180 out of the 183 electoral votes in the free states. The election results angered southerners. Without carrying a single southern state, Lincoln had still managed to win the presidency. The presidential election signaled that the South was losing its national political clout.

Lincoln intended to let slavery die out. People in the South believed that their economy and way of life would be destroyed if this happened. Just four days after Lincoln's election, South Carolina's legislature held a special convention to consider secession, formally withdrawing, from the Union. South Carolina was the first state to dissolve "the union now subsisting between South Carolina and other States."

Southerners noted that the original states had voluntarily joined the Union. Surely, they reasoned, states could also exit. Mississippi, Florida, Alabama, Georgia, Louisiana, and Texas followed South Carolina's example and seceded from the Union. These former states formed the Confederate States of America. Its new constitution guaranteed the right to own slaves.

STANDARDS PRACTICE

DIRECTIONS Read each question and circle the letter of the best response.

3 What did the election of 1860 signal to the South?

A that there were too many political parties
B that the South was losing its national power
C that Southern votes had not been counted
D that Lincoln had stolen the presidency

4 Why did states think that they should be allowed to secede from the Union?

A because Lincoln did not carry any of the southern states
B because Lincoln was not legally elected
C because states had voluntarily joined the Union
D because staying in the Union would destroy their way of life

History–Social Science Grade 8 Standard 8.10.4

STANDARDS REVIEW

HSS 8.10 Students analyze the multiple causes, key events, and complex consequences of the Civil War.

8.10.4 Discuss Abraham Lincoln's presidency and his significant writings and speeches and their relationship to the Declaration of Independence, such as his "House Divided" speech (1858), Gettysburg Address (1863), Emancipation Proclamation (1863), and inaugural addresses (1861 and 1865).

During his campaign for the United States Senate in 1858, Abraham Lincoln talked about the *Dred Scott* case. In this case, the Supreme Court ruled that enslaved African Americans were not citizens. Lincoln said that African Americans were "entitled to all the natural rights" listed in the Declaration of Independence. He specifically mentioned "the right to life, liberty, and the pursuit of happiness."

When Lincoln was sworn in as president in 1861, seven states had already left the Union. In his inaugural address, Lincoln tried to convince southerners that the federal government would not provoke a war. He hoped that, given time, southern states would return to the Union. The South did not respond to Lincoln's call for unity. Instead, Confederate officials took over many federal mints, arms storehouses, and forts. Lincoln vowed to hold on to Fort Sumter, at the entrance to Charleston Harbor in South Carolina. Before sunrise on April 12, 1861, Confederate guns opened fire on Fort Sumter. It was the beginning of the Civil War. States had to decide whether to secede or stay in the union. Federal troops were sent into the border states, those between the North and the South, to help keep them in the Union.

STANDARDS PRACTICE

DIRECTIONS Read each question and circle the letter of the best response.

1 Lincoln believed that African Americans were entitled to

A civil rights.
B legal rights.
C natural rights.
D none of the above

2 How did Lincoln keep border states in the Union?

A by bribing them
B by sending in federal troops
C by allowing them to free their slaves
D by taking over federal mints, arms storehouses, and forts there

STANDARDS REVIEW

On January 1, 1863, after more than eighteen months of civil war, Lincoln issued the Emancipation Proclamation. It was a military order that freed slaves in areas controlled by the Confederacy, but not in the border states, which Lincoln wanted to keep in the Union. Lincoln felt that the Emancipation Proclamation would help the North end the war. The proclamation went into effect that day, January 1, 1863.

The North suffered many defeats in the war, but their victory at the Battle of Gettysburg in 1863 was a major turning point. The South would never again be able to launch an attack on the North. The victory at Gettysburg took place on the same day that troops led by General Grant captured Vicksburg and took control of the Mississippi River.

Over 50,000 men died at Gettysburg. On November 19, 1863, Lincoln delivered the Gettysburg Address at the dedication of a cemetery at the battlefield. This address is one of the most famous speeches in American history. Lincoln reminded his listeners that the war was being fought to preserve the ideals of liberty, equality, and democracy, ideals spelled out in the Declaration of Independence.

On January 31, 1865, at Lincoln's urging, Congress proposed the Thirteenth Amendment, which made slavery illegal throughout the United States. It was ratified and took effect on December 18, 1865.

The Civil War ended on April 9, 1865. President Lincoln wanted to reunite the nation as quickly as possible. He had proposed a plan for readmitting the southern states even before the war ended. The issue of how the South would rejoin the Union remained unresolved when Lincoln was assassinated on April 14, 1865.

STANDARDS PRACTICE

DIRECTIONS Read each question and circle the letter of the best response.

3 The Emancipation Proclamation

A ended slavery in the United States.

B freed slaves in the border states.

C freed slaves in the Confederacy.

D gave African Americans the right to vote.

4 The Thirteenth Amendment

A ended slavery in the United States.

B freed slaves in the border states.

C freed slaves in the Confederacy.

D gave African Americans the right to vote.

STANDARDS REVIEW

HSS 8.10 Students analyze the multiple causes, key events, and complex consequences of the Civil War.

8.10.5 Study the views and lives of leaders (e.g., Ulysses S. Grant, Jefferson Davis, Robert E. Lee) and soldiers on both sides of the war, including those of black soldiers and regiments.

When the Confederate States of America was formed, the delegates elected Jefferson Davis of Mississippi as president of the Confederacy. Davis had hoped to be the commanding general of Mississippi's troops. He responded to news of his election with pained silence.

Robert E. Lee came from a wealthy Virginia family. He had led troops in the Mexican War. When the Civil War began, President Lincoln asked Lee to lead the Union Army. Lee declined and resigned his commission in the U.S. Army. He then became a general in the Confederate army.

Ulysses S. Grant was born in New York. A graduate of West Point, he too had served in the Mexican War. When the Civil War broke out, Grant joined the Union army. He soon became the most important figure in the war in the West. By September 1861 Lincoln had made him a general. Grant's strength in battle set him apart. Following the Siege of Vicksburg, Lincoln transferred Grant to the East and gave him command of the Union Army. After the war, Grant rode a wave of popularity to become president of the United States.

STANDARDS PRACTICE

DIRECTIONS Read each question and circle the letter of the best response.

1 Who was Lincoln's first choice to lead Union troops?

A Jefferson Davis
B Robert E. Lee
C Ulysses S. Grant
D none of the above

2 Who was the most important figure in the war in the West?

A Jefferson Davis
B Robert E. Lee
C Ulysses S. Grant
D Abraham Lincoln

STANDARDS REVIEW

For both Union and Confederate soldiers, the war was a challenge. They faced the violence and fear of the battlefield and the boredom of camp life. Soldiers spent most of their time dealing with hazards other than those of the battlefield. For every day of fighting, soldiers spent weeks living in uncomfortable and unhealthy camps. They faced bad weather, boredom, disease, and unsafe food. Thousands on both sides died of illness or unsanitary conditions. Nearly twice as many soldiers died of disease than died in combat.

For soldiers in combat, battle conditions were horrible. Fresh recruits were generally eager to fight. Experienced troops knew better. Fighting for every inch of ground, soldiers were killed by the thousands. Doctors and nurses in the field saved many lives, but many soldiers had legs and arms amputated to stop infection. Many who had only minor wounds died from infection.

From the beginning of the war, African Americans served in the Union army. At first, they were only allowed to serve as laborers. Enslaved African Americans who had escaped also joined the Union army. There were units of free African American soldiers in Louisiana and Kansas. By spring of 1863 African American units fought in the field with the Union army. They quickly showed that they could fight as well as any other unit.

About 180,000 African Americans served with the Union army during the war. They faced even greater danger than white troops. Instead of capturing African American soldiers, Confederate troops often killed them or sold them into slavery.

STANDARDS PRACTICE

DIRECTIONS Read each question and circle the letter of the best response.

3 What did most Civil War soldiers die of?

A gunshot wounds
B starvation
C disease
D bayonet wounds

4 When did African American units start fighting with the Union army?

A at the beginning of the war
B by spring of 1863
C shortly before the war's end in 1865
D after the Emancipation Proclamation

History–Social Science Grade 8 Standard 8.10.6

STANDARDS REVIEW

HSS 8.10 Students analyze the multiple causes, key events, and complex consequences of the Civil War.

8.10.6 Describe critical developments and events in the war, including the major battles, geographical advantages and obstacles, technological advances, and General Lee's surrender at Appomattox.

The Civil War began on April 12, 1861 when Confederate troops opened fire on Fort Sumter. Fort Sumter was a federal fort that controlled the entrance to Charleston Harbor in South Carolina. After 34 hours of battle, the fort surrendered to the Confederacy.

Each side, the North and the South, had advantages. The North had a larger population, most of the nation's factories, and a better network of railways. The South had a strong military tradition that provided many skilled officers.

Union general Winfield Scott's plan was to destroy the South's economy with a naval blockade of southern ports, to take control of the Mississippi River to divide the Confederacy, and to attack Richmond, Virginia, the Confederate capital. The Confederacy's strategy was to defend itself and wear down the Union's will to fight. It also hoped to capture the nation's capital, Washington, D.C. Confederate president Jefferson Davis hoped to use cotton to help him win foreign allies.

The first major clash between the two armies took place in July 1861. Northern troops were heading toward Richmond. They were met by southern troops headed by General Thomas "Stonewall" Jackson some 30 miles outside Washington, D.C. The South's victory at the First Battle of Bull Run dashed Union hopes of quickly winning the war.

STANDARDS PRACTICE

DIRECTIONS Read each question and circle the letter of the best response.

1 What advantages did the South have in the Civil War?

A a larger population
B skilled officers
C most of the nation's factories
D better transportation

2 The Confederacy planned to win the war by

A blockading northern ports.
B taking control of the Mississippi River.
C destroying the North's economy.
D wearing down the Union's will to fight.

STANDARDS REVIEW

The South hoped to take away the Union's advantage at sea with a new type of warship, ironclads. These ships were heavily armored with iron. The Confederates had turned a captured Union warship, the *Merrimack*, into an ironclad and renamed it the *Virginia*. The Union responded with its own ironclad, the *Monitor*. The two ships fought, but neither was seriously damaged. However, the days of wooden warships powered by wind and sails were coming to an end.

The Battle of Shiloh in 1862 was another early major battle. At first, the Confederates pushed the Union army back. But General Ulysses S. Grant ordered his troops to hold their ground. A hard-fought Union victory gave the Union greater control of the Mississippi River valley.

The Battle of Gettysburg in Pennsylvania in 1863 was a turning point in the war. General Robert E. Lee's troops would never again launch an attack in the North. The Union victory at Gettysburg took place on the same day that General Grant captured Vicksburg, in Mississippi.

U.S. President Abraham Lincoln transferred Grant to the East and gave him command of the Union army. In early 1864, Grant forced Lee to fight a series of battles in Virginia that stretched Confederate soldiers and supplies to their limit.

General William Tecumseh Sherman carried out the Union plan to destroy southern railroads and industries. He led his troops south from Tennessee in the spring of 1864. Sherman practiced total war, cutting a path of destruction through the heart of the South. In early April 1865 Sherman closed in on the last Confederate defenders in North Carolina. On April 2 Lee was forced to retreat from Richmond. On April 9, 1865, Lee surrendered to Grant at Appomattox Courthouse, Virginia.

STANDARDS PRACTICE

DIRECTIONS Read each question and circle the letter of the best response.

3 What was an ironclad?

A a kind of contract
B an early tank
C an armored ship
D none of the above

4 What was a turning point of the Civil War?

A the Battle of Bull Run
B the Battle of Shiloh
C the Battle of Gettysburg
D the Siege of Vicksburg

STANDARDS REVIEW

HSS 8.10 Students analyze the multiple causes, key events, and complex consequences of the Civil War.

8.10.7 Explain how the war affected combatants, civilians, the physical environment, and future warfare.

Both the Union and Confederate armies faced shortages. Armies were short of all supplies, including clothing, food, and even rifles. Most troops did not have standard uniforms. They simply wore their own clothes. Eventually, each side chose a distinct color for their uniforms. The Union chose blue and the Confederacy chose gray. Still, most soldiers had to provide their own shoes and winter coats.

Soldiers spent most of the time dealing with hazards other than those found on the battlefield. For every day of fighting, they spent weeks living in uncomfortable and unhealthy camps. Thousands of soldiers on both sides died of sickness brought on by illness and unsanitary conditions. Nearly twice as many soldiers died of disease as died in combat.

Civilians on both sides helped the war effort. They raised money, provided aid for soldiers and their families, and ran emergency hospitals.

STANDARDS PRACTICE

DIRECTIONS Read each question and circle the letter of the best response.

1 What kinds of uniforms did soldiers wear at the beginning of the Civil War?

A Union soldiers wore blue, and Confederate soldiers wore gray.
B Union soldiers wore gray, and Confederate soldiers wore blue.
C There were no standard uniforms.
D Both sides wore uniforms provided by their families.

2 How did civilians help the war effort?

A They raised money.
B They provided aid for soldiers' families.
C They ran emergency hospitals.
D all of the above

STANDARDS REVIEW

Dr. Elizabeth Blackwell, the first woman to earn a medical license, helped convince President Abraham Lincoln to form the U.S. Sanitary Commission in June 1861. Its tens of thousands of volunteers sent bandages, medicines, and food to Union army camps and hospitals.

Staff and volunteers also worked to keep Union troops healthy. Approximately 3,000 women served as nurses in the Union army. Doctors and nurses in the field saved many lives. However, antibiotics had not yet been invented and many soldiers had legs and arms amputated in order to stop infection from spreading through their bodies. Sometimes these surgeries were performed without anesthetics. Many soldiers with only minor wounds died from infection.

The physical environment did not escape damage. General William Tecumseh Sherman carried out the Union plan to destroy southern railroads and industries. He led his troops south from Tennessee in the spring of 1864. Sherman practiced total war, cutting a path of destruction through the heart of the South. He ordered his troops to destroy railways, bridges, crops, livestock, and other vital resources. They burned and pillaged plantations and towns, and freed slaves.

The Civil War saw the introduction of a new type of warship, ironclads. These ships were heavily armored with iron. The Confederates turned a captured Union warship, the *Merrimack*, into an ironclad and renamed it the *Virginia*. The Union responded with its own ironclad, the *Monitor*. The two ships fought, but neither was seriously damaged. However, the days of wooden warships powered by wind and sails were coming to an end.

STANDARDS PRACTICE

DIRECTIONS Read each question and circle the letter of the best response.

3 Who was Elizabeth Blackwell?

- **A** a nurse
- **B** a teacher
- **C** the first woman to earn a medical license
- **D** the director of the U.S. Sanitary Commission

4 How was the physical environment changed by the Civil War?

- **A** Canals were dug for transportation and dikes were built to block harbors.
- **B** Railways, bridges, crops, and plantations were destroyed.
- **C** both A and B
- **D** neither A nor B

STANDARDS REVIEW

HSS 8.11 Students analyze the character and lasting consequences of Reconstruction.

8.11.1 List the original aims of Reconstruction and describe its effects on the political and social structures of different regions.

Reconstruction was the process of reuniting the nation after the Civil War and rebuilding the southern states without slavery. Reconstruction lasted from 1865 to 1877. Southern soldiers returned home to find the world they had known before the war was gone. Cities, towns, and farms had been destroyed. The South's economy was in ruins. Many people faced starvation. Confederate money was worthless.

President Abraham Lincoln wanted to reunite the nation as quickly as possible. Others wanted to penalize the South. The only thing Republicans agreed upon was abolishing slavery. Slavery still existed in the border states, and many people feared that federal courts might someday overturn the Emancipation Proclamation.

In 1867 Congress passed the first of several Reconstruction Acts. The South was divided into five districts. Each district was controlled by a military commander. To be readmitted to the Union, a state had to write a new state constitution supporting the Fourteenth Amendment and giving African American men the right to vote.

Many northern-born Republicans moved to the South after the war. Some of them wanted to help formerly enslaved people. Others hoped to make money while rebuilding the southern economy. More than 600 African Americans were elected as representatives to state legislatures, and sixteen were elected to the United States Congress.

STANDARDS PRACTICE

DIRECTIONS Read each question and circle the letter of the best response.

1 What Reconstruction goal did all Republicans agree on?

A military occupation of the South
B punishing the South
C abolishing slavery
D all of the above

2 What did a state need to do to be readmitted to the Union?

A write a new constitution
B support the Fourteenth Amendment
C give African American men the right to vote
D all of the above

STANDARDS REVIEW

HSS 8.11 Students analyze the character and lasting consequences of Reconstruction.

8.11.2 Identify the push-pull factors in the movement of former slaves to the cities in the North and to the West and their differing experiences in those regions (e.g., the experiences of Buffalo Soldiers).

Following the Civil War, African Americans in the South were free, but they continued to face severe discrimination. Economic opportunities for African Americans in the South were extremely limited. Educational opportunities were limited in the South as well. These factors tended to "push" African Americans out of the South. In 1879, thousands of African Americas migrated from the South and moved north to Kansas and other western states.

In the 1890s, African Americans from the rural South began moving to northern cities to seek industrial jobs. They hoped to escape discrimination and find better economic and educational opportunities by leaving the South. Conditions and opportunities in the North tended to "pull" African Americans from the South to the North and West.

STANDARDS PRACTICE

DIRECTIONS Read each question and circle the letter of the best response.

1 In moving north, what were African Americans trying to escape?

A jobs
B discrimination
C better educational opportunities
D all of the above

2 What did African Americans from the rural South hope to find in northern cities?

A jobs
B economic opportunities
C educational opportunities
D all of the above

STANDARDS REVIEW

HSS 8.11 Students analyze the character and lasting consequences of Reconstruction.

8.11.3 Understand the effects of the Freedmen's Bureau and the restrictions placed on the rights and opportunities of freedmen, including racial segregation and "Jim Crow" laws.

The Freedmen's Bureau was an agency that was established to provide relief for poor people in the South. It distributed food to the poor and provided education and legal aid for freed people. It also assisted African American war veterans. The Freedmen's Bureau played an important role, helping to establish more schools in the South. Most freed people had never learned to read or write because of laws against educating enslaved African Americans. The Bureau also helped establish several universities for African Americans.

Soon after the Civil War ended, every southern state had passed Black Codes, or laws that greatly limited the freedom of African Americans to sign work contracts. This created working conditions very similar to those under slavery. African Americans who stayed on plantations often became sharecroppers. Most of them ended up living in a cycle of debt, never achieving true financial freedom.

After Democrats regained control in the South, many states set up a poll tax in an effort to deny the vote to African Americans. They also introduced legal segregation, or forced separation of whites and African Americans in public places. These laws were referred to as Jim Crow laws. The Supreme Court ruled that enforced segregation was constitutional if "separate-but-equal" facilities were provided.

STANDARDS PRACTICE

DIRECTIONS Read each question and circle the letter of the best response.

1 What was the most important result of the Freedmen's Bureau?

A It provided jobs.
B It provided medical care.
C It established schools.
D It built housing.

2 What was the Supreme Court's ruling on Jim Crow laws?

A The laws were morally wrong.
B Segregation was legal if separate-but-equal facilities were provided.
C The laws were unconstitutional.
D It refused to hear Jim Crow cases.

STANDARDS REVIEW

HSS 8.11 Students analyze the character and lasting consequences of Reconstruction.

8.11.4 Trace the rise of the Ku Klux Klan and describe the Klan's effects.

Following the Civil War, African Americans were elected to office. One result was that resistance to Reconstruction increased among the majority of white southerners. Many white southerners disapproved of African American officeholders. One Democrat noted, "'A white man's government' [is] the most popular rallying cry we have."

In 1866, a group of white southerners in Tennessee created the Ku Klux Klan. This secret society opposed civil rights, particularly suffrage, for African Americans. The Klan used violence and terror against African Americans. The group grew and quickly spread throughout the South. Klan members wore robes and disguises to hide their identities. They attacked and even murdered African Americans, white Republican voters, and public officials.

Local governments and police did little to stop the violence. Many officials feared the Klan or were sympathetic to its activities. In 1870 and 1871, the federal government took action. Congress passed laws that made it a federal crime to interfere with elections. It also made denying citizens equal protection under the law a federal crime.

Within a few years, the threat posed by the Klan had been greatly reduced. But groups of whites continued to assault African Americans and Republicans throughout the 1870s.

STANDARDS PRACTICE

DIRECTIONS Read each question and circle the letter of the best response.

1 Who were the members of the Ku Klux Klan?

A African American office holders
B scalawags
C supporters of civil rights
D opponents of civil rights

2 What did Congress do in response to the Ku Klux Klan's activities?

A It passed laws making it a crime to interfere with elections.
B It passed laws to deny citizens equal protection under the law.
C It outlawed the wearing of robes in public.
D It outlawed the Republican Party.

Name ______________________ Class ______________ Date ______________

STANDARDS REVIEW

HSS 8.11 Students analyze the character and lasting consequences of Reconstruction.

8.11.5 Understand the Thirteenth, Fourteenth, and Fifteenth Amendments to the Constitution and analyze their connection to Reconstruction.

Reconstruction was the process of reuniting the nation and rebuilding the southern states without slavery. The Emancipation Proclamation only freed enslaved African Americans in Confederate states not occupied by Union forces. Slavery was allowed to continue in Union-controlled states. Many people feared that the federal courts might someday declare the Emancipation Proclamation unconstitutional. On January 31, 1865, at President Lincoln's urging, Congress proposed the Thirteenth Amendment, making slavery illegal in the United States.

Many Republicans worried about what would happen when the southern states were readmitted to the Union. Fearing that the Thirteenth Amendment might be overturned, Republicans proposed the Fourteenth Amendment in the summer of 1866. It overturned the *Dred Scott* decision and granted citizenship to all people born in the United States (except Native Americans). The Fourteenth Amendment also guaranteed citizens equal protection of the laws.

The Fifteenth Amendment gave African American men the right to vote. It went into effect in 1870 and was one of the last major Reconstruction laws passed at the federal level.

STANDARDS PRACTICE

DIRECTIONS Read each question and circle the letter of the best response.

1 Which amendment was passed to ensure that the Emancipation Proclamation would not be declared unconstitutional?

A the Thirteenth Amendment
B the Fourteenth Amendment
C the Fifteenth Amendment
D none of the above

2 Which amendment guaranteed citizens equal protection of the laws?

A the Thirteenth Amendment
B the Fourteenth Amendment
C the Fifteenth Amendment
D none of the above

STANDARDS REVIEW

HSS 8.12 Students analyze the transformation of the American economy and the changing social and political conditions in the United States in response to the Industrial Revolution.

8.12.1 Trace patterns of agricultural and industrial development as they relate to climate, use of natural resources, markets, and trade and locate such development on a map.

After the Civil War, settlers began to move to the Great Plains and other western lands. Gold and silver discovered in Nevada and Colorado attracted people from all over the world. Cattle ranches grew up on the Great Plains. This area eventually became known as the Cattle Kingdom. Ranchers grazed huge herds on public land called the open range. These lands had once been home to Plains Indians and buffalo herds. Farmers began to buy range land and build fences.

A Second Industrial Revolution took place in the late 1800s. It was a period of rapid growth in U.S. manufacturing. Some of the most important advances in technology took place in the steel industry. These advances allowed production to grow rapidly, lowering the cost of steel.

As the price of steel dropped, so did the cost of building railroads. Companies built thousands of miles of new steel track. Manufacturers and farmers sent products to market faster than ever by rail. Cities where major rail lines crossed, such as Chicago, grew rapidly. Railroads helped spur western growth. As rail travel and shipping increased, railroads and related industries began employing more people.

STANDARDS PRACTICE

DIRECTIONS Read each question and circle the letter of the best response.

1 What contributed to the growth of the cattle industry?

A fencing of land
B growth of railroads
C opening of ranch land
D all of the above

2 What industry developed rapidly due to the drop in the cost of steel?

A the mining industry
B the shipping industry
C the automotive industry
D the railroad industry

History–Social Science Grade 8 — Standard 8.12.2

STANDARDS REVIEW

HSS 8.12 Students analyze the transformation of the American economy and the changing social and political conditions in the United States in response to the Industrial Revolution.

8.12.2 Identify the reasons for the development of federal Indian policy and the wars with American Indians and their relationship to agricultural development and industrialization.

As miners and settlers began crossing the Great Plains in the mid-1800s, they pressured the federal government to provide greater access to western lands. To protect these travelers, U.S. officials sent agents to negotiate treaties with the Plains Indians. Treaties were signed that accepted Native American claims to most of the Great Plains. These treaties also allowed the United States to build forts and roads and permitted travel across Native American homelands. The U.S. government promised to pay for any damages to Indian lands.

The discovery of gold in Colorado brought thousands of miners to the West. They soon clashed with the Plains Indians. In 1861, new treaties set aside reservations. Native Americans were supposed to stay on these reservations, which made hunting for buffalo and other traditional customs almost impossible. When gold was discovered in the Black Hills of the Dakotas, the United States government insisted that the Sioux sell their reservation land there. Fighting soon broke out. The Battle of Little Bighorn was the worst defeat the U.S. Army suffered in the West. It was also the Sioux's last major victory.

STANDARDS PRACTICE

DIRECTIONS Read each question and circle the letter of the best response.

1 Under early treaties with Great Plains Indians, what did the federal government promise?

- **A** free education
- **B** free health care
- **C** free housing
- **D** to pay for damages to Indian lands

2 What happened when the federal government insisted the Sioux sell their reservation land in the Black Hills?

- **A** The Sioux moved peacefully.
- **B** The Sioux were sent on a forced march out of the Dakotas.
- **C** The Sioux fought Army troops.
- **D** Fighting broke out between Indian tribes.

Name ______________________ Class ______________ Date ______________

History–Social Science Grade 8 Standard 8.12.3

STANDARDS REVIEW

HSS 8.12 Students analyze the transformation of the American economy and the changing social and political conditions in the United States in response to the Industrial Revolution.

8.12.3 Explain how states and the federal government encouraged business expansion through tariffs, banking, land grants, and subsidies.

In the early days of the United States, Alexander Hamilton wanted to encourage new forms of economic growth. He also wanted to promote manufacturing and business. One way of promoting industry was to pass high protective tariffs. These taxes raised the prices of foreign products and caused Americans to buy U.S-made goods. Tariffs led to regional conflicts. Northern manufacturers wanted tariffs to protect their industries from foreign competition. Southerners, who imported their manufactured goods, opposed tariffs. Protective tariffs helped the North, but they impacted southern farmers.

Hamilton wanted to start a national bank where the government could safely deposit its money. The bank would also make loans to the government and businesses. Although he had originally opposed it, when Thomas Jefferson became president, he agreed to let the National Bank of the United States function as it had under the Federalists.

In order to encourage the building of a transcontinental railroad to connect the East to the West, the federal government passed the Pacific Railway Acts in 1862 and 1864. These acts gave railroad companies loans. Companies were also given large land grants that could be sold to pay for construction costs. By 1872, Congress had granted more than 131 million acres of public land to railroad companies. In exchange, the government asked the railroads to carry mail and troops at lower rates.

STANDARDS PRACTICE

DIRECTIONS Read each question and circle the letter of the best response.

1 Why did Hamilton want tariffs?

A to anger the South
B to anger Thomas Jefferson
C to make money for himself
D to promote manufacturing

2 How did Congress help railroad companies?

A by providing labor to build tracks
B by supervising the construction
C by giving them land grants
D by paying higher rates for carrying U.S. mail and troops

Name ______________________ Class ______________ Date ______________

History–Social Science Grade 8 — Standard 8.12.4

STANDARDS REVIEW

HSS 8.12 Students analyze the transformation of the American economy and the changing social and political conditions in the United States in response to the Industrial Revolution.
8.12.4 Discuss entrepreneurs, industrialists, and bankers in politics, commerce, and industry (e.g., Andrew Carnegie, John D. Rockefeller, Leland Stanford).

Andrew Carnegie focused his efforts on steelmaking, and he expanded his business by buying out competitors when steel prices were low. By 1901, his mills were producing more steel than all of Great Britain's steel mills combined. Carnegie lowered production costs by owning the businesses involved in each step of the manufacturing process, a system known as vertical integration.

John D. Rockefeller started an oil-refining company. By 1870, his Standard Oil Company was the largest oil refiner. Rockefeller also used vertical integration. In addition, he used horizontal integration, which meant that he owned all the businesses in a certain field. By 1880, his companies controlled 90 percent of the U.S. oil refining business.

Leland Stanford made enormous sums of money selling equipment to miners in California. While he was governor of California, he became one of the founders of the Central Pacific railroad. He also founded the college known today as Stanford University. Later in his life he came to believe that industries should be owned and managed by their workers.

Carnegie, Rockefeller, Stanford, and other business leaders gave away large amounts of money. By the late 1800s, various charities had received millions of dollars from philanthropists.

STANDARDS PRACTICE

DIRECTIONS Read each question and circle the letter of the best response.

1 Which entrepreneur used both horizontal and vertical integration?

A Andrew Carnegie
B John D. Rockefeller
C Leland Stanford
D none of the above

2 Which entrepreneur believed that industries should be owned and managed by the workers?

A Andrew Carnegie
B John D. Rockefeller
C Leland Stanford
D all of the above

History–Social Science Grade 8

STANDARDS REVIEW

HSS 8.12 Students analyze the transformation of the American economy and the changing social and political conditions in the United States in response to the Industrial Revolution.

8.12.5 Examine the location and effects of urbanization, renewed immigration, and industrialization (e.g., the effects on social fabric of cities, wealth and economic opportunity, the conservation movement).

During the late 1800s people moved to cities in record numbers, resulting in rapid urban growth. Some city residents were skilled workers, but many more were poor laborers. As new farm equipment reduced the need for farm labor, large numbers of rural residents moved to the cities. In addition, new immigrants settled in large cities.

Stronger and cheaper steel, along with new devices such as the safety elevator, led to the development of skyscrapers. Mass public transit systems eased traffic flow. Many urban areas, however, were not ready for their rapid population growth. Growth often led to shortages in affordable housing. Overcrowded and unsanitary tenements were often packed together in areas close to factories. Fire and crime were common problems. Reform efforts of city governments were often limited by internal corruption or lack of funds. Many middle-class Americans who could afford to moved away from cities and into the suburbs.

Reformers tried to solve the problems caused by fast industrial and urban growth. The movement for urban reform led to new professions, such as city planning and civil engineering. In time, zoning laws, safer building codes, improved transportation, and better sanitation improved city life.

STANDARDS PRACTICE

DIRECTIONS Read each question and circle the letter of the best response.

1 What was one of the causes of the rapid urban growth of the late 1800s?

A development of skyscrapers
B new immigrants
C mass transit
D overcrowded housing

2 Which of the following problems was most closely associated with overcrowding in cities?

A unsanitary conditions
B corruption
C new technology
D industrial growth

STANDARDS REVIEW

HSS 8.12 Students analyze the transformation of the American economy and the changing social and political conditions in the United States in response to the Industrial Revolution.

8.12.6 Discuss child labor, working conditions, and laissez-faire policies toward big business and examine the labor movement, including its leaders (e.g., Samuel Gompers), its demand for collective bargaining, and its strikes and protests over labor conditions.

The Second Industrial Revolution was a period of rapid growth in U.S. manufacturing. Factory machines that could be run by unskilled workers replaced the jobs of skilled craftspeople. Low-paid factory workers needed little training and were easily replaced. They feared that if they complained about pay or poor working conditions, they would lose their jobs. Workers began to form labor unions to try to improve working conditions. Union leaders wanted better wages and working conditions for workers. They believed that by using collective bargaining, workers had a greater chance of winning labor disputes.

The American Federation of Labor (AFL), led by Samuel Gompers, organized national unions. The AFL tried to get better wages, hours, and working conditions for laborers. One way of doing this was to go on strike. In May 1886, thousands of union members in Chicago went on strike to gain an eight-hour workday. During the strike, violence erupted. Several people were killed and 100 others were wounded. This event became known as the Haymarket Riot. Eight people were arrested and convicted of conspiracy. In general, government tended to support big business over labor unions.

STANDARDS PRACTICE

DIRECTIONS Read each question and circle the letter of the best response.

1 Unions tried to get better working conditions by

A negotiating with the government.
B collective bargaining.
C holding job fairs.
D replacing supervisors.

2 What position did the government tend to take in disputes between workers and big business?

A It supported workers.
B It supported unions.
C It supported business.
D It tried to remain neutral.

STANDARDS REVIEW

HSS 8.12 Students analyze the transformation of the American economy and the changing social and political conditions in the United States in response to the Industrial Revolution.

8.12.7 Identify the new sources of large-scale immigration and the contributions of immigrants to the building of cities and the economy; explain the ways in which new social and economic patterns encouraged assimilation of newcomers into the mainstream amidst growing cultural diversity; and discuss the new wave of nativism.

During the late 1800s, immigrants came to the United States by the millions. However, immigration patterns had changed, and many of these new immigrants came from southern and eastern Europe. Many were looking for better economic opportunities. Others, such as Armenians and Jews, were escaping political or religious persecution.

Many new immigrants had worked on farms in their homelands, but they were unable to buy land in the United States. Instead, they found jobs in the cities, where most of the country's manufacturing took place. They often had no choice but to take low-paying, unskilled industrial jobs in the construction, garment, or steel industries. Many immigrants moved into neighborhoods with others who came from the same country. In these neighborhoods they could hear their own language, eat familiar foods, and keep their traditional customs.

Anti-immigrant feelings grew in the late 1800s. Many "nativists" held racial and ethnic prejudices against immigrants. In some places, nativists took part in violence against immigrants. Others worked for the passage of laws to stop or limit immigration.

STANDARDS PRACTICE

DIRECTIONS Read each question and circle the letter of the best response.

1 Where did most new immigrants find work?

A in unskilled industrial jobs
B on farms
C as skilled craftspeople
D on the railroads

2 What was a nativist?

A a person born in the United States
B an immigrant living in the United States
C a person who supported immigration
D a person who was opposed to immigration

STANDARDS REVIEW

HSS 8.12 Students analyze the transformation of the American economy and the changing social and political conditions in the United States in response to the Industrial Revolution.

8.12.8 Identify the characteristics and impact of Grangerism and Populism.

More farmland and greater productivity led to overproduction. This led to lower prices for crops. Some farmers lost their farms and homes. Many became tenant farmers, working land that belonged to someone else. By 1880, one fourth of all farms were rented by tenants, and the numbers kept growing. Many farmers blamed businesspeople, particularly railroad owners, for their economic woes. As economic conditions worsened, farmers began to form associations to protect and to help their interests. The National Grange was formed in 1867. It was a social and educational organization for farmers. The Grange campaigned for political candidates who supported farmers' goals. It also called for laws to regulate rates charged by railroads. In February 1877 the Supreme Court ruled that the government could regulate the railroads. In February 1887 Congress created the Interstate Commerce Commission to ensure fair rates on railways.

To gain political power, many farmers organized to elect candidates that would support their cause. These organizations became known as the Farmers' Alliances. In 1892 they formed the Populist Party. It called for the government to own the railroads, telephone, and telegraph systems. The Populists also backed an eight-hour workday and limits on immigration. The 1896 presidential election, however, marked the end of both the Populist Party and the Farmers' Alliances.

STANDARDS PRACTICE

DIRECTIONS Read each question and circle the letter of the best response.

1 Why did the National Grange form?

A to help businesspeople
B to help the railroads
C to help farmers
D to limit immigration

2 Which of the following was a goal of the Populist Party?

A private ownership of railroads
B eliminating limits on immigration
C private ownership of telegraph systems
D an eight-hour workday

Name ______________________ Class ______________ Date ______________

History–Social Science Grade 8 — Standard 8.12.9

STANDARDS REVIEW

HSS 8.12 Students analyze the transformation of the American economy and the changing social and political conditions in the United States in response to the Industrial Revolution.

8.12.9 Name the significant inventors and their inventions and identify how they improved the quality of life (e.g., Thomas Edison, Alexander Graham Bell, Orville and Wilbur Wright).

Thomas Edison looked for possible uses of electricity. His research center in Menlo Park, New Jersey, came to be called an invention factory. Thomas Edison took a practical approach to science and eventually held more than 1,000 patents on inventions. Edison also built a power plant to supply electricity, making electric lighting possible.

In 1876, Alexander Graham Bell patented the telephone. Bell was a Scottish-born speech teacher who studied the science of sound. The telephone revolutionized communication. By 1880 there were about 55,000 telephones in the United States, and by 1900 there were almost 1.5 million.

In 1876, a German engineer invented an engine powered by gasoline. In 1893, Charles and J. Frank Duryea built the first practical automobile in the United States. By the early 1900s, thousands of cars were being built in the United States.

Orville and Wilbur Wright were bicycle makers who were fascinated with the possibility of flying. The brothers built a lightweight airplane with a small gas-powered engine. In Kitty Hawk, North Carolina, Orville Wright made the first piloted flight in a gas-powered plane on December 17, 1903.

STANDARDS PRACTICE

DIRECTIONS Read each question and circle the letter of the best response.

1 Which inventor's research center was called an invention factory?

A Alexander Graham Bell
B Thomas Edison
C Orville Wright
D none of the above

2 What did the Wright brothers do before they invented the airplane?

A They were speech teachers.
B They worked in an automobile factory.
C They built bicycles.
D none of the above

4500631223
Printed in the United States of America